Intimate Moments With God

An Experience in Prayer, God's Language of Love

Valentine A. Rodney

For conferences, workshop, crusades, conventions, and seminars, contact:

Rev. Valentine Rodney
c/o Word Impact Ministries International
P.O. Box 787
Spanish Town
St. Catherine
Jamaica

Email: varodney@gmail.com

Tel: Jamaica: 876 390 2303 | USA: 407 545 5052

Cover Design by Dayton Lydner (colourssignsandgraphics@gmail.com)

Published by:

ISBN: 978-1-965635-25-4 (paperback)
**   978-1-965635-26-1 (hardback)**

Scripture quotations marked (NLT) are taken from the Holy Bible, New Living Translation, copyright © 1996, 2004, 2007 by Tyndale House Foundation. Used by permission of Tyndale House Publishers, Inc., Carol Stream, Illinois 60188. All rights reserved.

First Edition: March 2025

This book is dedicated to all believers everywhere who have a burning and urgent desire to experience greater intimacy in their daily walk with God through prayer.

Acknowledgments

I am deeply indebted to God, our Father, and the Lord Jesus Christ for providing the inspiration that has resulted in this book.

Like Paul the Apostle, I have not completely mastered what I have written about, but I still felt compelled to motivate and inspire others on this intimate journey called prayer. I am doubly sure that the Holy Spirit played a pivotal role in superintending these writings, which will have a positive benefit and a tsunami-like impact on the lives of countless readers.

About the Author

Bishop VALENTINE A. RODNEY, BSc, MA., is an international speaker whose ministry has taken him to the USA, Canada, Europe, Africa, and several countries within the Caribbean, where he has also fostered and facilitated ministerial training and developmental programs. He has done undergraduate work at the University of the West Indies in Marine Biology and Graduate work in Missions at the Caribbean Graduate School of Theology. Bishop Rodney has served in the areas of Christian Education, Evangelism, Leadership Development, Prayer and Intercession, Youth Ministry, Radio and Television, and Pastorate. He is also actively involved in welfare programs and mentorship to men, youths, and ministers. He is a strong advocate for Christian Transformational Development where the church interfaces with the community and assists in strategic intervention that is both redemptive and empowering.

He is the author of several books, including "Shameless Persistence: The Audacity of Purposeful Praying," "A Way of Escape: How To Handle The Tests And Temptations Of Life," "The Power of the Secret Place: The Place Of Relationship, Resolution And Revelation," and "Prescription For Healthy Relationships: A Practical Guide To Overcoming Offences."

Bishop Rodney is the host and presenter of the television program, Word Impact, aired on MTM tv, and the online program, Let's Talk, a weekly study program viewed on Facebook and YouTube. After going through a life-threatening situation in 2024, Bishop released two new books titled, "Show Me The Evidence: Miraculous Displays Of God's Power In Critical Times" and Giving Up Is Not An Option: Persevering Despite Life's Challenges."

Bishop Rodney is an International Instructor for Walk Thru The Bible Ministries, Director for Word Impact Seminar Events (WISE), and the Director of Word Impact Ministries International, a non-denominational ministry that caters to the empowerment of the Christian Community and the salvation of the lost. He is an International Chaplain and Ambassador with Covenant International University and Seminary. His Motto is *"Go Where There Is No Path and Leave a Trail."*

VALENTINE A. RODNEY is married to Yevett for over twenty-eight years. Their union has produced two daughters, Zharia and Ana-Olivia.

Table of Contents

Introduction

Prayer was inaugurated by God as a means of maintaining active communication between man and Himself. It represents both a time to fellowship with and converse with God. Prayer provides an opportunity for man to spend intimate moments with God as he seeks to know God in the measure that He will reveal Himself. Prayer therefore is both a journey and a great adventure. In it, the infinite and omnipotent God is pleased to allow finite man to spend quality time with Himself.

Man must recognize that these moments were never designed to instruct God on how to conduct His affairs, but rather that man would make himself available to submit to and obey his Creator. God does not forbid asking questions or venting when we are on an emotional roller coaster. He, however, needs our undivided attention so we can hear what He has to say. Prayer is more about listening to God than to our own voices talking.

God wants us to understand that prayer is the great facilitator of intimacy. These moments spent with Him must be riveting and engaging. The moments must never be rushed or hurried but flow at the pace that He so desires. We come with anticipation and expectation because no two interactions are the same. He knows so much about us and wants to share so much with us that we must consider this our highest priority and most treasured moments.

God desires to be the last person on our minds before we retire to sleep at night and the first when we awaken. We are important to Him, and He must be the priority in our lives. The times we spend with God must never be likened to a chore or some drudgery. We are forever excited and take joy in our interaction because He fills our lives with meaning and embraces us with His love.

For the LORD your God is living among you. He is a mighty savior. He will take delight in you with gladness. With his love, he will calm all your fears. He will rejoice over you with joyful songs." (Zephaniah 3:17 - NLT).

This book is a treasure trove that details the importance of prayer as the real and dynamic intimate connection with God. For far too long, many have been consumed with the request side of prayers as it relates to the acquisition of material things, and now, we need to remember that there is a deeper and far more intentional association that God requires. God desires more than just hearing what we need; He needs us. We must connect with Him in terms of body, soul, and spirit. We are uniquely His and must respond to Him with our whole hearts, souls, and minds.

I trust that these pages will awaken a resolve on the inside that will consume us with the kind of passion where we miss

God at the end of each prayerful engagement and are anxious to reconnect with Him urgently thereafter. Let us be aware of the pivotal role the Holy Spirit plays in all of this. It is Him who will guide us into all truth as we follow His leading and engage in meaningful conversations with God.

When the Spirit of truth comes, he will guide you into all truth. He will not speak on his own but will tell you what he has heard. He will tell you about the future. (John 16:13 - NLT).

As the intimate bond and connection is established with God through prayer, this profound sense of peace and serenity will permeate our entire being. A deeper sense of spiritual awareness will accompany this as we become conscious of and embrace His will as ours. We refuse to be daunted or discouraged in this spiritual pursuit, for the sovereign God has made Himself completely available to us.

The unique bonding experience is one that we will cherish for a lifetime, knowing that this far outweighs all human relationships. Our personal growth becomes enhanced as our values and behaviour align with His as we become progressively attuned to what being intimate with God is all about.

Growing in intimacy with God will provide a great sense of security as we bask in the knowledge that He hears us and will guide us appropriately based on His omniscience.

Intimacy through prayer with God now becomes our main priority in seeking after Him.

Through our prayerful interaction with Him, we gain strength for adversity and the challenging times ahead. We therefore trust His plan and provisions for our lives. The principles undergirding spiritual intimacy through prayer are to be cherished and put into practice to ensure longevity in our relationship with God.

Too often, there is a request culture that seems to trump relational intimacy to the point where we love to receive but not to give. Intimacy is about mutual giving and receiving. Let us therefore break out of the stereotypic role and reflect the true nature of God in giving ourselves to Him as He has made Himself available for us. It is true that intimacy with God will provide a deep understanding of self and inner peace, purpose, and the knowledge that God loves and cares for us always.

We must always remember that intimacy can never be about spending time with oneself. Even when engaged in the practice of discipline, our solitude is certainly not to be alone but rather to designate a time to spend with God in meditation, conversation, and conscious reflection.

Chapter One

Naked And Unashamed

Now the man and his wife were both naked, but they felt no shame. (Genesis 2:25 - NLT).

Every manufacturer that builds a product will have a purpose for their creation. Most products that are available for sale will often come as standard with an instruction or operational manual. Though quickly discarded in most instances, the manual provides invaluable information concerning product type and usage. The eternal God has ensured that humanity would have a manual that speaks to their origin and purpose. Only the competent authority is authorised to speak concerning all aspects related to the product.

Man is indeed the product of God's sovereignty and creative prowess. If we must access knowledge concerning man, then reference must be made to the manual called the Bible. Man, who is referred to as the crowning jewel of God's creation, exists to fellowship and commune with God. He was meant to interact and not be divorced from God and His presence.

"You are worthy, O Lord our God, to receive glory and honour and power. For you created all things, and they exist because you created what you pleased." (Revelation 4:11 - NLT).

In the original design and construction of Adam, God wired him for communication with Himself. It is reported that regular meetings took place in the Garden of Eden during the cool of the day. This was not just to facilitate instructions regarding the garden's management but also for man to have fellowship or communion with God.

Before the initial trespass, there was no need for man to hide from God or for any attempt to miss those moments of interaction with God in the Garden of Eden. By his own free volition, man enjoyed the quality moments he spent with God. There was no cowardly fear but only holy reverence and a desire to be in close communion. Each conversation with God was fulfilling as the sovereign God of the universe was aware of how to communicate with one of the crowning jewels of His creation, man.

Vulnerability is a vital key to spiritual intimacy. We are therefore vulnerable, open, and transparent before God because we trust Him completely and wholeheartedly. Intimacy thrives in an atmosphere where the consideration for betrayal does not exist. We have confidence in a God who is truly our most trusted confidant.

With transgression came an obvious disconnect between man and God. The hiding among the trees was an attempt to distance themselves from God to avoid interacting with Him. Sin definitely affects our ability to be open and transparent. We must face the consequences of our choices rather than attempt to avoid them. This was futile as God still reached out to man who was clearly not where he should have been. Forgiveness, love, and healing can restore and reconnect. What is lost can be regained through redemption if we earnestly seek after it.

When the cool evening breezes were blowing, the man and his wife heard the LORD God walking about in the garden. So they hid from the LORD God among the trees. Then the LORD God called to the man, "Where are you?" He replied, "I heard you walking in the garden, so I hid. I was afraid because I was naked." (Genesis 3:8-10 - NLT).

This phrase, *"naked and unashamed,"* is said to represent the innocence of a relationship between two people who are one with each other and God. *"Naked and unashamed"* refers to the idea of approaching God in prayer with complete openness and vulnerability, without hiding any flaws or sins, fully trusting in God's love and forgiveness. It is essentially presenting oneself before God as you truly are, without shame or pretence; it signifies a deep level of honesty and reliance on God's grace in prayer.

Like Adam and Eve before the fall, we come before this relational God aware of our failures and shortcomings but

17

knowing that these are neither permanent nor insurmountable obstacles to Him. We have heeded His invitation to come, knowing that His Word and presence are truly transformational.

God's love and acceptance are based on the finished work of Christ on the cross, and His eternal love for us facilitates this measure of vulnerability and willingness on our part to bare all to Him. We come freely to God with no preconceived inhibitions or fear of rejection. Completely exposed, we appear before Him, confident that we can reveal our true selves through prayer, which is the most intimate of all expressions. We hold nothing back in the baring of our hearts and souls, relying upon Him for strength, sustenance, and guidance.

Even though we have failed God, He is more willing to redeem and accept rather than reject and condemn us. The call will always be for us to come and draw close to Him in all humility. God desires more to pardon and embrace rather than to isolate us. Intimate fellowship ranks high on His order of priorities.

Nothing in all creation is hidden from God. Everything is naked and exposed before his eyes, and he is the one to whom we are accountable. (Hebrews 4:13 - NLT).

God is God enough to deal with all that we bring to Him in prayer. We have the unconditional assurance of His continued favour and abiding presence with us. He will actively work on our transformation so that the bonds of intimacy can be renewed.

Give all your worries and cares to God, for he cares about you. (1 Peter 5:7 - NLT).

Before God, we can share our anxieties, struggles, and desires without hesitation or fear. Not only does He want to hear, but He is also available to help. The God we serve is both dependable and reliable. With Him, we can afford to be genuine and honest, not having to filter out thoughts and emotions but simply speaking from the depths of our hearts.

"Naked and unashamed" is the very essence of repentance, which challenges us to lay ourselves bare before God with the confidence that He is faithful and just and will not condemn us but offer the kind of forgiveness that heals. He will not hurt us but will help us, especially in this time of vulnerability and need. God will never make a promise that He will not fulfil. He has a proven track record and will meet us at the point of our need. As we reach out to Him, He will pick us up and give us a firm footing for our faith that will not go unrewarded.

"Come now, let's settle this," says the LORD. "Though your sins are like scarlet, I will make them as white as snow. Though they are red like crimson, I will make them as white as wool." (Isaiah 1:18 - NLT).

Let us trust God completely as He transforms us fully into His original intended design. The intimacy and oneness that we seek are available as we come through the doors of repentance. The power of repentance lies in the removal of shame brought about through transgression. As we confess to God, there is an acknowledgment of our failures and failings and a willingness to trust Him for true freedom. Repentance is therefore liberating and is a virtue of our openness and vulnerability in prayer.

That inner yearning and longing was always anticipated by God and reflects how man was wired through creation. The loneliness that man feels and experiences is a precursor for the intimacy to which man is called to experience with God. The desire for intimacy with God is in man, but man must make a choice to foster its development through fervour and commitment.

A common way to distinguish guilt from shame is to say that guilt is about what you have done, and shame is about who you are. The presence of these does not in any way mean that we cannot be reconciled to God. Honesty and humility are important facets to the reestablishment of what was previously lost. No matter what we have done, we are never outside of the scope of His reach.

So let us come boldly to the throne of our gracious God. There we will receive his mercy, and we will find grace to help us when we need it most. (Hebrews 4:16 - NLT).

Chapter Two

The Awakening of the Heart

S piritual awakening is not only needed; it is required for there to be a renewal of the relationship that God truly desires. We will never be passionate about what we do not love. Only God can stir the heart's longing to engage with Him in the most private and intimate of settings. This desire can be compared with but never quite equal to that of thirst and hunger. The soul will push that desire beyond the scope of human vocabulary yet within the reach of the rich rewards of true intimacy with the Creator.

The "awakening of the heart for God" refers to a spiritual experience where individuals recognize and respond to God's presence and love, often marked by a renewed sense of purpose and connection undergirded by intense prayer. This awakening can lead to a surrender of one's heart to God, trusting in His goodness, and seeking His guidance. It can also foster a sense of intimacy and closeness with God. An awakened heart for God often manifests as a desire to love and serve others, reflecting God's love and compassion.

Evidently, what the soul longs for needs to be formally acknowledged and submitted to. There is a level of incompleteness and sheer emptiness that accompanies the distancing of the soul from its ultimate source, who is God.

The awakening of the soul is an initiative of God to bring awareness and the passionate pursuit of that which can only result in the satisfaction of that inner longing that every man ultimately craves after, though indescribable at times but nevertheless refreshing and fulfilling. We can attempt to exist without but will never truly have lived until the fears are abandoned and the connection secure.

The awakening is the spark triggered by the Creator who knows and reveals Himself to be acknowledged and for us to share in the abundant life that only He can bestow. Intimacy, though involving the intellect, is not purely intellectual but the heart's response to a benevolent God.

The bane of our existence is tied to our rebellion and unwillingness to seek after God, who has made Himself available through divine disclosures. The real tragedy of death is embedded in our separation from Him, who gave us life and is the bedrock of our existence.

An intimate moment with God refers to a deeply personal and meaningful experience where we avail ourselves of the connection and communion with Him. This will allow us to feel His all-embracing love and proximity as we truly understand our own vulnerabilities but remain resolute in our complete trust and submission to Him. These are moments when a personal relationship is cultivated beyond mere religious rituals as we share His heart and receive guidance and comfort from Him.

These moments are characterised by heartfelt convictions and a deep sense of connection that is mainly on a spiritual plain, even though it may include physical expressions. We truly become transparent, open, and honest with respect to our thoughts, feelings, and struggles. It requires us to be patient, open, and honest concerning our innermost thoughts and feelings to Him. We are then conscious that active listening must take place as we embrace the inner peace He provides and are inspired and even motivated by His words. These intimate moments are very much up close and personal, being totally unique to everyone.

Intimate moments with God will involve reading and meditating upon the scriptures, engaging in praise and worship from the depths of our hearts, soul-searching introspection, and generally sharing with God from the heart. There is such an overwhelming sense of fulfilment that is experienced the greater the level of intimacy that we share with God.

We cannot hide from the fact that true devotion and intimacy with God will require heart-felt repentance as our lives are aligned with His will and His Word. Distancing ourselves from evil and cleaving to what is good is a sure key to real intimacy with God. We must give up those things that displease Him, and then give in to Him as we follow and enjoy His ways.

Search me, O God, and know my heart; test me and know my anxious thoughts. Point out anything in me that offends you, and lead me along the path of everlasting life. (Psalm 139:23-24 - NLT).

We are still learning the depths of intimacy, so with unquestioned loyalty, we grant Him permission to the inner recesses of our hearts. Nothing is hidden from Him in this most sacred of all moments. We desire to be stripped of all aspects of rebellion and pride and wholly surrendered to Him. We are anxious for Him to teach us His ways and are already committed to walking in it because our hearts safely trust Him.

The raging inferno of intimacy is fuelled by a trust that minimises the likelihood of potentially offensive situations. However, intimacy with God allows us to heal as He reveals. We are constantly and consistently giving of ourselves, and as He is, so shall we be. The more we bond with God, the greater the shared interests we develop. The more we engage with God the less of self or flesh is exposed.

Intimacy with God requires boldness and is life-translational. As we experience Him more, we are transformed into His glory by His Spirit.

O God, you are my God; I earnestly search for you. My soul thirsts for you; my whole body longs for you in this parched and weary land where there is no water. (Psalm 63:1 - NLT).

Waiting on and listening to God are crucial elements towards developing intimacy with God. This will require patient endurance coupled with rapt attention. We must never miss Him in this season of searching.

In those days when you pray, I will listen. If you look for me wholeheartedly, you will find me. (Jeremiah 29:12-13 - NLT).

Trust in the LORD with all your heart; do not depend on your own understanding. Seek his will in all you do, and he will show you which path to take. (Proverbs 3:5-6 - NLT).

True intimacy with God is the antidote for worry, fear, and anxiety. We must involve Him daily in all aspects of our lives. We never exclude Him from any of our affairs. He is interested in the great things and the tiniest necessities of life. Nothing ever escapes or evades His watchfulness. His eyes are continually upon the righteous, and His ears are open even to the faintest of their cries.

Don't worry about anything; instead, pray about everything. Tell God what you need, and thank him for all he has done. Then you will experience God's peace, which exceeds anything we can understand. His peace will guard your hearts and minds as you live in Christ Jesus. (Philippians 4:6-7 - NLT).

God expects not only devotion but wholehearted trust in Him. Our perception of God can directly influence how passionately we engage with Him. Prayer is a divine initiative that requires our partnership. God is pleased to call us alongside Himself to explore the vast reservoir of a relationship with Him. Prayer is not a destination but a heartfelt response to God's invitation to come and dwell with Him.

Chapter Three

The Prayer Closet and the War Room

"When you pray, don't be like the hypocrites who love to pray publicly on street corners and in the synagogues where everyone can see them. I tell you the truth, that is all the reward they will ever get. But when you pray, go away by yourself, shut the door behind you, and pray to your Father in private. Then your Father, who sees everything, will reward you. "When you pray, don't babble on and on as the Gentiles do. They think their prayers are answered merely by repeating their words again and again. Don't be like them, for your Father knows exactly what you need even before you ask him!" (Matthew 6:5-8 - NLT).

These well-used but often conflicting approaches to God can either enhance or reduce our interactions with the Creator to the mere servicing of our needs but not necessarily the accomplishment of His will. Our motive in approaching God is crucial and is basically a reflection of our heart. It is important to acknowledge that belief determines behaviour.

Though well-intentioned, the advent of the war room has upset the apple cart of intimacy with God. In many spaces, we have traded that desire to know Him with enlisting God as either a serial killer or just a weapon within our arsenal to be used to justify our desire for revenge on those who have hurt us.

I do believe there is a space and place for passionate engagement with God as we seek the protection that only He can afford from the ongoing assaults by the enemy. But may we also remember that a part of the warfare revolves around the enemy endeavouring to resist our desire to intimately bond with our God. I am not in any way suggesting that we ignore the threat nor the reality of war but simply find a respite to connect for some and reconnect for others that intimacy with God. Never allow the noise of the battle to put a strain on our relationship with God.

Could it be that through the war room, we have found a way to attempt to coerce God into our will being done rather than His? This has certainly not enhanced our spirituality but rather turned the believers into spiritual terrorists, often devoid of empathy and compassion. We may see God as a warrior through the war room but not know Him as a friend.

I am not in any way ignorant of the evils that permeate society and its potential impact on us, but rather stoutly resisting the notion that our prayers must always reflect this warlike disposition. Much time must therefore be spent in knowing and seeking after God.

The war room has become that place, not for bonding or building a relationship with God, but rather to lead an assault against enemy lines. The author will acknowledge the presence of evil and the need for spiritual warfare but question the over-preoccupation, with spiritual warfare being the primary reason for our engagements and interactions with God. This can reduce the moments we spend with God to simply rebuking, decreeing, and declaring rather than in humility and reverence, trusting and knowing Him. When we approach God in prayer, it is never to order Him around or give Him instructions but to listen intently to what He has to say and to be submissive to His will.

Prayer must once more become that space where we lay our hearts bare before the sovereign potentate with reverence and devotion. When did prayer become this place of perpetual conflict and arrogant meddling?

Love for God and humanity is what characterises the prayer closet. Its existence is an indelible reminder that God desires more bonding than bombing. Knowing God intimately will cause intercession to flow as our love for humanity and His will strengthens.

The sermon on the mount speaks to this call to intimacy and is uniquely referenced by the prayer He taught His disciples to pray. The conversation began with an acknowledgment of the close-quartered relationship that humanity shares with God to the extent that He is called Father. God is Creator, and we derive our existence from Him.

We therefore approach God from a relational standpoint where He is seen as source, Father, protector, provider, and guide. Intimacy revolves around our stated dependency and reliance upon Him. We endeavour to trust Him completely and be completely honest and open in our approach.

The prayer closet represents both a call and an invitation to meet with God in the corridors of our hearts. God is already where we are endeavouring to be. The idea of a prayer closet speaks to privacy and intimacy. This can be a physical space dedicated to communion with God or simply the inner recesses of our hearts. This is where the demands and noises of the outside world are silenced because of the intense focus demanded. This space is both personal and private, and it is just simply for two. We enter by faith and dwell based on desire.

The prayer closet is your spiritual storehouse where all that you need from God in accordance with His will is accessible and readily available. It is the place of respite, trust, and confidence. It is where the weary soul can rest, and those wounded by the attacks of the enemy and the cares of life can be restored. There, we are both unashamed and unafraid.

We can afford to be real and transparent as we venture into this up close and personal space. This is the place where we hide nothing, being fully aware that we are in the presence of Him who knows all things. This is where we acknowledge who we are and come face to face with His self-revelation and spiritual disclosures.

Nothing in all creation is hidden from God. Everything is naked and exposed before his eyes, and he is the one to whom we are accountable. (Hebrews 4:13 - NLT).

In the prayer closet, we meet with God on His terms and conditions. There is a heightened level of vulnerability but absolutely no fear. His love for us becomes both a cloak and a canopy that is both reassuring and affirming. We are allowed to have frank and open discussions, even to the point of venting before Him. The prayer closet or secret place only has room for two: the Lord and the seeker. In the prayer closet, we lose our independence, exchanging it for wholehearted dependency on Him.

Distractions are minimised, if not completely silenced, as we set aside or reserve this time only for Him. This is not the place for the door to be kept open so that things can compete or vie for our attention. The worries and cares of this life are not allowed to invade the privacy of this space, for they are locked out as we close the mental and emotional doors of our minds and hearts. We are then truly shut in with Jesus in this secret place.

The prayer closet was never meant for us to be totally isolated continuously from the outside world; it was a place where we could frequently meet up with God as we share with Him the most intimate details of our lives. Intimacy building requires us to put up the "do not disturb" sign. We will be momentarily unavailable to all human interactions as we seek God in earnest.

The prayer closet is the place where we know and acknowledge His revealed will for our lives. It is a place where our trust will never be violated, and we are free from the accusations of the adversary. Let me also humbly submit that the prayer closet is mobile. We can connect with God anywhere and anytime. Jesus' words to the Samaritan woman are very instructive and must be given serious consideration. Our access to God is never tied to only one place or location; rather, it is limitless, for we can meet up with Him wherever we are. The most important criterion is that each encounter be done from the depths of our being (i.e., out of our spirit). There is simply no excuse for there to be no intimacy with God. The trek is more a spiritual than a physical one. Jesus is truly only a prayer away.

Jesus replied, "Believe me, dear woman, the time is coming when it will no longer matter whether you worship the Father on this mountain or in Jerusalem. You Samaritans know very little about the one you worship, while we Jews know all about him, for salvation comes through the Jews. But the time is coming—indeed it's here now—when true worshipers will worship the Father in spirit and in truth. The Father is looking for those who will worship him that way. For God is Spirit, so those who worship him must worship in spirit and in truth." (John 4:21-24 -NLT).

Even though the prayer closet can often refer to a physical location, it is not limited to that. It transcends the physical and is more representative of that spiritual space where we shut in and connect with God. Simply put, this now becomes the inner recesses of our hearts—a place where we become unbothered by the distractions of life. This inner sanctum of our heart preserves the intimacy that is reserved for only two: you and the Lord Jesus.

He is held in the highest esteem and with true honour and reverential respect. We are willing to share all our concerns and care. Nothing is too small or too great. There is such a magnitude of sufficiency in Him that allows us to lean wholeheartedly upon Him, sharing and baring all.

So humble yourselves under the mighty power of God, and at the right time he will lift you up in honor. Give all your worries and cares to God, for he cares about you. (1 Peter 5:6-7 - NLT).

Let us be aware that God is already in the prayer closet awaiting our arrival or indeed us being conscious of His presence. He is the one who personally invites us into this space for regular periods of interaction. The beauty of the secret place is that we are talking with a God we cannot see and who will offer tangible benefits that we can see. The private moments will yield public rewards just as He has promised. The secret place is not for occasional but frequent visits. Once we enter, we submit to His timing. The secret place is such that we can have a private moment in a public space.

The prayer closet represents that place where we can hear the still, small voice of God in the quietness and solitude of our hearts. Don't just search for the dramatic and the spectacular but rather the supernatural. The shutting of the closet door is never to keep Him out but rather to keep us in with Him. The benefits that can be derived when we maintain our focus are amazing. The prayer closet truly distances us from the hustle and bustle of life's activities and provides clarity and consciousness. God speaks, but we are required to pay attention through effective listening. It is truly illegal to pray and not expect God to respond.

The prayer closet or secret place is a safe space where we can afford to bare all and share all, experiencing the heights of vulnerability during our time of disclosure. It is here that we not only build and develop a personal relationship with God but also, in earnest, seek His unconditional will for our lives. The prayer closet represents that space where we get rid of all the things that have cluttered our lives as we await God's significant input into our lives.

The prayer closet is indeed the place of transformation and revelation. It is a place of divine exchange where we experience God's best for our lives. Even though the

34

invitation is extended, our consent is needed for participation and partnership. This is the place for a face-to-face encounter and not necessarily a stand-off. God requires us to yield or surrender as we experience so much more of Him. This is not the place for resistance or rebellion but submission and compliance. As we become unclothed from the things that He abhors, we are now clothed with His righteousness and glory.

The prayer closet is the space that we retreat to, especially when we have been pressed by the cares of this life and need to be reassured of God's abiding presence. When we are battle-weary and brought to the point of physical and spiritual fatigue, we can find rest and refreshing for our souls. In the privacy of our communion with Him in the prayer closet, restoration and healing take place.

The prayer closet or secret place is a place where we are covered by God and held secure. His voice will cause our fears and anxieties to dissipate like vapour into nothingness. Here, the distress and cares of this life are cast off as we actively commune with God and receive the needed help. We will discover the vastness of God's resourcefulness in this private (inner) room. His supplies are limitless and cater to every form of human need.

It is amazing how these private moments with God can yield an abundance of public successes as He responds to our requests. We are asking a sovereign God for the manifestation of supernatural results. We become acutely conscious and aware of His will and our desires and ultimately yield to His will. Like Jesus in the Garden of Gethsemane, we cannot relinquish our responsibility to pray. It is inevitable that we see through the manifestation of God's will for our lives, irrespective of the personal cost to us. We therefore stand resolute and determined that we live a surrendered life in keeping with His will.

"Father, if you are willing, please take this cup of suffering away from me. Yet I want your will to be done, not mine." (Luke 22:42 -NLT).

The prayer closet is not a place of manipulation or coercion but submission to God's will, irrespective of how we may initially feel. Partnering with God in this space will allow us to begin to see things from His perspective, so armed with this revelation, we promote His will. Once we know the direction He is steering us into, our prayer becomes far more focused and earnest in our entreaty. We are now able to announce with much clarity and confidence the manifest will of God and knowingly walk in the realm of answered prayer.

God's response is indeed inevitable for those who will spend time with Him. We recognise that our prayers do not have to be obvious for the results to be significant. We cannot, at times, avoid others seeing us praying, but we are not praying to be seen by men. Prayer was never meant to increase visibility among men but rather to improve intimacy with God.

It is a given that the prayer closet gives us time to interact with God so we will know and embrace His will for our lives. As we commit to pray, He is already committed to respond. We will have the evidence of private prayers yielding public response.

Chapter Four

Intimacy and Hypocrisy

"When you pray, don't be like the hypocrites who love to pray publicly on street corners and in the synagogues where everyone can see them. I tell you the truth, that is all the reward they will ever get." (Matthew 6:5 - NLT).

The great obstacle to intimacy in prayers is pretending. Jesus calls this level of pretense hypocrisy. The hypocrisy of which Jesus speaks is likened to stage acting within a theatre. Rest assured that God knows who you are, so there is certainly no need for us to be disingenuous. Sincere prayer is far more than what is said from the lips and must include what is acknowledged and felt in the heart.

In prayer, the ultimate focus must be on God, and we have to avoid the noise of distraction. Jesus was adamant that true intimacy must resonate from the heart. It is not how much you say but what is said from the heart. We need to discourage the practice of being so focused on praying right that we disconnect from God. Remember, we are simply not attempting to impress God with words but rather draw close to Him with heart.

"When you pray, don't babble on and on as the Gentiles do. They think their prayers are answered merely by repeating their words again and again." (Matthew 6:7 - NLT).

Since God is omniscient, He cannot be tricked by misrepresentation. He hears the words from our lips but knows our heart's condition. Sincerity is truly the precursor to intimacy. This encompasses both words and deeds. This is the expression of one to another from a deep place within.

It is who you are and the way you live that count before God. Your worship must engage your spirit in the pursuit of truth. That is the kind of people the Father is looking for: those who are simply and honestly themselves before Him in their worship. God is sheer being itself—Spirit. Those who worship Him must do it out of their very being, their spirits, their true selves, in adoration (see John 4:23-24).

It is the spirit in man that connects to God by way of the Holy Spirit. This is indeed the highest expression of intimacy that any human being can be involved with. No earthly relationship can compare to this response.

We are admonished in the scriptures not to be hypocritical in our prayers. Hypocrisy, Jesus stated, involves the offering of prayers publicly to receive the acknowledgment of men. There is nothing wrong to be seen praying; however, we should not pray to be seen. The focus in this level of hypocrisy is not God but men. If God is our focus in prayer, then we will give Him due regard and reverence. He will be the subject of our conversation. We should be far more passionate about being heard by God than men.

The true challenge therefore lies in whom we are desirous of hearing us. We are explicitly forbidden to pray for the applause of men but rather for the acknowledgment of God. It is therefore not how men see us but rather how God views us.

Mere repetition of learned phrases does not constitute the type of prayers God seeks. The endless babble associated with Gentile behaviour is clearly not endorsed by Jesus. There must be clarity and coherency. Prayer must never be turned into a theatrical production where the emphasis is on people and their response to us but not on the response from God. Prayer is not meant to showcase our talent but rather to converse with God.

Role-playing in prayer lacks sincerity as we pretend to be what we are not. Praying to appear devoted does not have the respect or the reward from God. The focus cannot simply be on what is being said but rather on who we are talking with. The language of prayer must involve not just words but sincerity of heart. It is not the loudness of your prayer that symbolises your devotion to God. It may however receive the praises of men but no attention from God if the motive is wrong. It is amazing that Jesus referred to the hypocrites as being those from the religious community comprised of the Scribes and the Pharisees. They were attention seekers rather than seeking after God. The shallowness of their prayer was reflected in it being self-centered and not God-centred. It is obvious that Jesus was not impressed by this approach to prayer and saw it as being false, lacking in humility, and not worthy of soliciting the attention of God.

Positioning ourselves merely to be seen by men is clearly a self-centered motive and does not fulfil the criteria of other-centered, which is required for prayer to be a meaningful engagement. This public display of prayer to announce so-called piety in a religious setting or public thoroughfare may appeal to men but does not deceive God in any way. It reeks of pride and clearly misrepresents what prayer is meant to be. This showboating in the name of prayer was irreverent and not endorsed by the one who inaugurated prayer. Both the motivation and attitude in prayer must be a clear reflection of a heart in the passionate pursuit of God.

Prayer cannot be reduced therefore to the spectacle of talking to God but relishing the approval of men. The most intimate expression of prayer is undergirded by the recognition that the audience is truly one person, who is God. The true reward for prayer lies in spiritual growth and closeness to God and not merely for human recognition. Hypocritical praying never truly acknowledges God as Father and is devoid of the bonding that is formed from drawing close to God. Whatever is done for show lacks humility, and the scriptures clearly state God's attitude towards the proud. Hypocritical praying is truly a case of self-deception in believing that God acknowledges this deplorable attitude.

And he gives grace generously. As the Scriptures say, "God opposes the proud but gives grace to the humble." (James 4:6 - NLT).

In the same way, you who are younger must accept the authority of the elders. And all of you, dress yourselves in humility as you relate to one another, for "God opposes the proud but gives grace to the humble." (1 Peter 5:5 - NLT).

While we utilise prayer points, we must never forget the point of prayer. The focus here must include effective listening and not only talking but moving from monologue to dialogue, where prayer becomes both engaging and meaningful. Remember that it is illegal to pray and not expect God to respond. God must have His say for prayer to be considered complete. Never ever forget the importance of listening to God, for this constitutes an important and vital aspect of prayer.

It would be a serious travesty to be esteemed by others as a deeply spiritual person based on the appearance of public devotion to praying but, in the same breath, to be rejected by God for a lack of sincerity. People being in awe of us or holding us in high esteem means nothing without the endorsement of God. God does not only listen to what is being said from our lips, but He also sees the condition of our hearts and is able to judge righteously.

But the LORD said to Samuel, "Don't judge by his appearance or height, for I have rejected him. The LORD doesn't see things the way you see them. People judge by outward appearance, but the LORD looks at the heart. (1 Samuel 16:7 - NLT).

It should not be that we are more inclined to pray publicly but not privately—fervency before a human audience but infrequent when it comes to personal time with God. Real hypocrisy lies in having an inadequate personal devotion life yet seeking to have a public impact with words in the public space. We need to be cautious and not just try to sound spiritual in our prayers when there is an audience. Prayers in private or before others are all deemed conversations with God and that must always be remembered to avoid the pull of hypocrisy.

The presence of witnesses and the location of the prayer are not the main issues that Jesus addresses in hypocritical praying. The clear purpose of Jesus is to critique those whose primary audience is the crowd and whose primary goal is maintaining or increasing their own spiritual reputation. I am in no way discounting the value of public praying but rather calling for an examination of one's motive. Care must be taken to avoid selfish preoccupation as we approach God in prayer.

Chapter Five

That I May Know Him

I want to know Christ and experience the mighty power that raised him from the dead. I want to suffer with him, sharing in his death. (Philippians 3:10 - NLT).

T hough often disputed, the inner longings of the soul cannot truly be disregarded with all honesty. It may not often be acknowledged, but it cannot be denied. It is a life experience to be treasured, for that is how we were wired by the Creator/Manufacturer. We all have as our default settings a desire for intimacy with God. This can never be fully erased, and the unwillingness to embrace it will only stir within us immense feelings of discomfort.

Knowing God must become man's number one priority. God is a relational God and has made Himself available so man can commune with Him at the deepest level. Man will only find his greatest sense of fulfillment when he is with God. There is no substitute for this aching and longing within. We are not here referring just to intellectual knowledge but knowing God within the sphere of the totality of our being.

"You are worthy, O Lord our God, to receive glory and honor and power. For you created all things, and they exist because you created what you pleased." (Revelation 4:11 - NLT).

It is imperative that we know God and not merely know about Him. We crave a firsthand rather than a secondhand experience. This will require us to converse with Him frequently. Conversation is an important building block in establishing and maintaining intimacy with God. In fact, God both desires and requires it. The more we know God, the greater the work of transformation that is effected within our hearts. Intimacy must never be confined to just the physical because it is a deeply spiritual endeavour requiring the totality of our being.

It is clear from the above text that man is uniquely wired to fellowship and commune with God. This, then, is inherently the reason for His creation.

This is not just some random conveyor belt of thoughts but rather a discerning approach to the main emphasis of prayer, which is intimacy with God. I trust that we will not equate these writings to the rambling of the ignorant or an author unaware of the current realities. I am in no way asking us to abandon the concept of spiritual warfare where there is the need to resist the enemy, but calling us to engage in drawing near to God.

And he gives grace generously. As the Scriptures say, "God opposes the proud but gives grace to the humble." So humble yourselves before God. Resist the devil, and he will flee from you. Come close to God, and God will come close to you. (James 4:6-8a - NLT).

The call to come close for communion and fellowship has resonated throughout the ages as God's ultimate desire for His people. God delivers you from so He can deliver you unto Himself. Deliverance removes the barriers and impediments to true fellowship with Himself.

You have seen what I did to the Egyptians. You know how I carried you on eagles' wings and brought you to myself. (Exodus 19:4 - NLT).

God's plan of redemption is intricately tied to His desire to have us for Himself. He frees us from bondage so we can connect and, in some cases, reconnect with Him. We are delivered to serve Him in Spirit and in Truth.

We must be publicly passionate about who we are privately intimate with. We must and should demonstrate PDA (Public Display of Affection) in our prayers and worship. Lack of fervency indicates a drought in intimacy. You cannot be deeply in love with whom you are not passionate about. It is time to reconcile our private devotional life to our corporate displays of seeking after God. The heart must throb with the passionate beat for true intimacy with God. This indeed must resonate within the core of our beings. Therefore, the yearning is to be closer than we have ever been with Him.

True intimacy is never devoid of responsibility and accountability. God will always hold up His end of the agreement. Our reverence and appreciation for God should cause us to sacrifice and be committed to this long-term relationship with Him.

If we are unfaithful, he remains faithful, for he cannot deny who he is. (2 Timothy 2:13 - NLT).

We rest solidly in the fact that God cannot be unfaithful. He is as good as His words to us. This makes Him both trustworthy and reliable. He will never promise and not fulfil. We must therefore trust in the answers that God provides, even when they are not quite what we were looking for. We trust that He knows what is best for us.

God is not a man, so he does not lie. He is not human, so he does not change his mind. Has he ever spoken and failed to act? Has he ever promised and not carried it through? (Numbers 23:19 - NLT).

The unchanging nature of God gives us confidence as we approach Him in prayer. He is not double-minded, and He demonstrates consistency in His dealings with us. There is however the need for patient endurance as we await the fulfilment of what God has already revealed in prayer.

For example, there was God's promise to Abraham. Since there was no one greater to swear by, God took an oath in his own name, saying: "I will certainly bless you, and I will multiply your descendants beyond number." Then Abraham waited patiently, and he received what God had promised. (Hebrews 6:13-15 - NLT).

Submission to God in prayer should cause us to be in full support of His agenda and be passionately committed to playing our part or role. Remember that prayer is the consummate partnership between humanity and divinity. This trust in and reliance on God goes way beyond mere intellectual assent. It is driven by a knowledge of God and His faithfulness to stand by His commitment to us. Challenges and obstacles will never be seen as contradicting what God has revealed through prayer, as He is willing to deal with the situation at hand. We therefore remain loyal by demonstrating total reliance upon Him. Prayer is the place where trust and confidence in God is acknowledged as we come to terms with His faithfulness based on experience and observation.

Chapter Six

The Rebirth of Prayer

Once Jesus was in a certain place praying. As he finished, one of his disciples came to him and said, "Lord, teach us to pray, just as John taught his disciples." (Luke 11:1 - NLT).

The observation made by the disciples based on the behaviour of those who modeled prayer was sufficient motivation for them to inquire concerning the mechanics of praying. Let us be aware that their request revolved around the how-to and the heart of praying. Jesus not only taught on prayer in the scriptures, but He modeled how prayer should be done. It was not just the words they heard, but that, matched with fervour and passion. They could not deny that what they saw they desired. Prayer is rooted not just in principles but also in the commitment to practice. It must move from observation to application. The great malady of this—and many ages—is not unanswered prayer but unoffered prayer.

My conviction is that prayer needs to go through a spiritual renaissance. In the area of prayer, too much is taken for

51

granted, and far too much is left undone. The rebirth of prayer here refers to a renewed and deepened commitment to prayer; this being the result of a significant shift in one's spirituality. Those involved will experience a fresh awakening in their relationship with God, underscored by a renewed commitment, zeal, and fervour in serving God wholeheartedly.

Prayer will once more become the central priority exemplified by transformed lives. Prayer then becomes more constructive and not merely a series of meaningless babel. The practice of prayer would become more consistent and engaging, underpinned by an unparalleled love for God and His mission.

I am in no way suggesting a total death of prayer but simply a dormancy that is creeping in, compounded by, in some areas, a general apathy and lethargy to this spiritual discipline.

The major tenets of such a spiritual encounter would incorporate:

— **Transformation:** This is a resultant change from a superficial to a deeper connection and intercourse with God. This would begin within (intrinsically) and move beyond the routine or superficial. This would be reflected both individually and corporately as those engaged become consumed by the desire for more of God. Like a raging inferno, this would have a wildfire effect as it spreads contagiously like a spiritual pandemic.

— **Personal Experience**: This results in a heightened level of awareness of God's presence and a deeper understanding and involvement in the discipline of prayer. The born-again experience that Jesus explained to Nicodemus is representative of what all believers go through. This will allow for a greater alignment of one's life to the will and purpose of God.

— **Intentionality:** One must be intentional in discovering the true meaning behind prayer and not just be advocates but those who are in relentless pursuit of a deep, spiritually rewarding experience with God. A more focused approach is taken, resulting in more meaningful conversations with God. This includes but is not limited to confessions, gratitude, and submission to and dependence on His guidance. As the scriptures are studied, greater insights are gained that will enrich the prayer life. A greater desire to witness and share one's experience in the faith will also become a priority for those whose lives have been so affected and influenced.

— **Spiritual Growth:** You can pray and not grow, but you can't grow spiritually and do not pray. The incorporation of the spiritual disciplines will facilitate the growth of the believing community as this is undergirded with prayer. The resultant spiritual growth would be marked by positive changes in attitude, interpersonal relationships, and decision-making. A deeper connection with God will result in stability emotionally, mentally, and spiritually.

Why Seek for a Rebirth in Prayer?

- Having experienced a period of spiritual dryness where one feels disconnected from God and has lost the meaning of the true importance of prayer in life.

- Significant life events, which may include a major transition or trauma that pushes one into a deep search for God and, by extension, His spiritual guidance.

- An intense longing that can only be filled through having an intimate relationship with God.

- Prompting by the Holy Spirit as He puts in your heart a desire for personal revival and global evangelism.

Hindrances to Effective Prayer (Prayerful Intimacy)

The hindrances mentioned below are like intimacy blockers that distance us from the vital relationship with God that we both treasure and seek.

- **Unconfessed Sin** – the tolerating and entertaining of sin is very detrimental to the intimacy we are endeavouring to build and renders our prayers ineffective. The antidote to this dilemma is confessing and forsaking (repentance) through which we obtain cleansing (see Psalm 66:18, 1 John 1:9).

- **Lack of Faith** – Trusting and believing are essential parameters that must be met. Mark 1:1-6 shows that unbelief was at the heart of the limited number of miracles wrought by Jesus in Nazareth. Doubting causes indecision and instability. When a person is of two minds, they will not approach anything with certainty. When we doubt, we relinquish our partnership with God and cease to become a beneficiary of His generosity (see James 1:6-8).

- **Disobedience** – This speaks to non-compliance to God and His Word. Whenever there is disobedience, it reeks of disloyalty, and that is always a dealbreaker for intimacy (see John 14:15, Luke 6:46, Ephesians 2:2, Acts 5:29, Isaiah 1:19).

- **Lack of Integrity** – Honest and strong moral principles underscore the foundation of intimacy in prayer. Lack of transparency delays healing and restoration and affects our ability to reach out to others based on their perception of us (see Proverbs 11:3, Proverbs 12:22, Psalm 119:1, Proverbs 10:9, Proverbs 11:3).

- **Unforgiveness** – If we make no allowance for weakness in others, this can seriously affect our relationship with God and others. Unforgiveness chains and imprisons and is a roadblock to true intimacy (see Matthew 6:14-15).

- **Wrong Motives** – This has to do with the reason why something is done (for example, selfless or selfish) (see James 4:3).

- **Idols in our lives** – Whatever we are more devoted to or hold in higher esteem than God (see Ezekiel 4:3).

The rebirth of prayer has to do with the rising popularity of prayer after a period when it was deemed unpopular based on a lack of participation and fervency in doing it.

Problem With Prayer

- The seen connecting with the unseen by faith.
- It requires dedicating time and patience.
- Only a priority when difficulties arise.
- Major responsibility to be borne by the seeker.
- Invasion of privacy.
- Seen as an obligation or a necessary chore.
- Unwillingness to change despite conviction.
- Fearful about not being considered normal.
- Lazy.

- Struggling with the prospect of submission and surrender.
- Tension between earnest prayer and fitting into the world.
- Not fully committed.
- Intensification of spiritual warfare with increased commitment to prayer.

Prayer Builds a Relationship with God – You cannot exclude personal intimacy from your desire to pray. It is extremely difficult to pray if you are relationally bankrupt. Our level of prayer is often directly proportional to our love for God. Prayer reveals God's dependability and reliability. He can be trusted on all accounts.

Prayer demonstrates our love for God – What you are devoted to and treat as a priority must mean something to you. Our love for God must characterize sincere prayer. We reverence Him but do not display a cowardly fear of Him. Whereas external factors may initiate prayers, the internal parameter of love will sustain them. Prayer is not just about words but heart. Whatever we say to God must come directly from our heartfelt commitment to Him. Prayer must emanate from a place deep within and flow naturally and normally.

"For God is Spirit, so those who worship him must worship in spirit and in truth." (John 4:24 - NLT).

Love allows for an easier flow of conversation. It also helps strengthen the bonds of intimacy. It is much easier to listen and make sacrifices when love is the bond that holds the relationship together. Because we love God, we are positive in our response to Him, knowing that He is concerned about our welfare. We place a value on what He has to say and certainly put a weight on our conversations. Love involves valuing the moments that are spent together and developing consistency in spending time with Him. It involves engaging and showing up where and when He needs us.

Honouring God in Prayer – We show due regard and respect by what we say and how we conduct ourselves. We are consistent in our praise and thanksgiving, noting that as a hallmark of our gratitude and devotion to Him. Honour requires us to be attentive and focused during these moments of prayer and not allow our thoughts to wander away from the purpose at hand. We not only request but are willing to follow His guidance and direction. We honour God in our prayer by not allowing distractions or anything else to compete with the quality time that we are spending with Him. It would be a disservice and a great dishonour if, after speaking with God, we fail to listen to His response. Remember always that God expects us to be ourselves in our approach to Him.

There can be no rebirth in prayer without turning to God with our whole heart, soul, and body. What has been lost must be regained, and the trust that leads to intimacy must be explored. All barriers erected must be torn down, and God must once more have the preeminence in our lives.

Therefore, say to the people, 'This is what the LORD of Heaven's Armies says: Return to me, and I will return to you, says the LORD of Heaven's Armies.' (Zechariah 1:3 - NLT).

Turning to God may require brokenness, repentance, and restitution. Because we seek to be renewed and for all outstanding matters to be rectified, we cry out to Him in response to His call to come. In such an intimate setting, we refuse to overlook any unresolved issue that may cause a disconnect or distancing. We come to reconnect by meeting all the requirements that He has set out.

The rebirth of prayer is contingent on the fact that we miss the fellowship we shared with Him and are anxious for the fires to be reignited through passionate engagement with God. The Word of God in us fuels those desires and makes connecting with Him all important. We overcome all natural desires in our search and pursuit of Him.

If you look for me wholeheartedly, you will find me. (Jeremiah 29:13 - NLT).

Like the believers in the early church, we will give ourselves over to prayer and the study of the Word of God.

Since the church is a spiritual organisation, its number one priority must be to God as they embrace the spiritual disciplines of prayer and the Word.

So the Twelve called a meeting of all the believers. They said, "We apostles should spend our time teaching the word of God, not running a food program. And so, brothers, select seven men who are well respected and are full of the Spirit and wisdom. We will give them this responsibility. Then we apostles can spend our time in prayer and teaching the word." (Acts 6:2-4 - NLT).

Jesus acknowledges unapologetically that one of the distinguishing features of the church must be prayer. Every local outpost must be characterized and identified by its commitment and dedication to prayer. This prayer initiative and support must be embraced and practiced by all who identifies with the Lord.

He said to them, "The Scriptures declare, 'My Temple will be called a house of prayer,' but you have turned it into a den of thieves!" (Matthew 21:13 - NLT).

Rebirth Requires Turning

Active communication with God will produce a holy boldness in communicating with Him despite the prevailing spiritual apathy in many regions. The call of God to turn to Him is explicit and requires our acknowledgment and surrender. Turning is contingent on our brokenness and submission to Him and His Word. Similarly, we must yearn for Him even as He yearns for us.

Therefore, say to the people, 'This is what the LORD of Heaven's Armies says: Return to me, and I will return to you, says the LORD of Heaven's Armies.' (Zechariah 1:3 - NLT).

It is important that we deal with all the intimacy blockers. None of them can be overlooked or not considered. Whatever caused the frigidity, rigidity, and hardness must go. All the outstanding issues must be finally settled. The disconnect and the rift will be healed as we heed the summons that He has made. With God's intervention comes a liberation and a cleansing. Having been purged, the internal obstacles no longer remain, and we freely give ourselves to Him.

It's your sins that have cut you off from God. Because of your sins, he has turned away and will not listen anymore. (Isaiah 59:2 - NLT).

One of the greatest deterrents to our spiritual intimacy with God is sin. We willingly acknowledge and repent for this so that the act of restoration can be completed. We are not only convicted but remorseful of what has broken His heart. With resolve and a grateful heart, we solicit His help in bridging the divide. As we bond with God, we not only desire but now possess His heart. Our desire for Him now surpasses all the basic needs of humanity. We refuse to be convicted and remain silent. We will speak with our lips what comes from our hearts pertaining to reconnecting with Him.

If you look for me wholeheartedly, you will find me. (Jeremiah 29:13 - NLT).

This is both a promise and a condition for our commitment. It is God rewarding our search for Him by making Himself available. This is not the God who hides but the one who reveals Himself. We can know nothing of God unless He is pleased to reveal that to us. We will not stop until there is this intimate engagement with Him based on our passionate pursuit of Him and His presence. This passionate engagement with God is aptly pictured in the song by Israel Houghton and New Breed, "Jesus at the Center" (2012).

We acknowledge that He is pivotal to our prayerful worship and praise. Him being at the centre is essential to the intimacy of our relationship.

Rebirth of Prayer in Response to Catastrophe

In the time of the prophet Joel, the major catastrophe described in the Bible was a devastating locust plague that ravaged the land of Judah, destroying crops and causing widespread famine, which Joel interpreted as a sign of divine judgment and a call for repentance from the people.

Prayer of Jehoshaphat: A Model of Trust and Dependency on God

O our God, won't you stop them? We are powerless against this mighty army that is about to attack us. We do not know what to do, but we are looking to you for help. (2 Chronicles 20:12 - NLT).

Total reliance on God is based on His sovereignty and a recognition of our humanity. Prayer is clearly the posture of dependency where we acknowledge our insufficiency and God's all-sufficiency. In prayer, we have a unique opportunity to express ourselves before an all-knowing God and seek both His wisdom and providential guidance. We see ourselves as limited but God as limitless. In prayer, we solicit God's divine help and assistance.

It is not that we think we are qualified to do anything on our own. Our qualification comes from God. (2 Corinthians 3:5 - NLT).

God must always be our first concern rather than our last resort. Having an intimate relationship with God in prayer provides the reassurance that God is listening and committed to action. God is both reliable and dependable, and we must approach Him with confidence.

So let us come boldly to the throne of our gracious God. There we will receive his mercy, and we will find grace to help us when we need it most. (Hebrews 4:16 - NLT).

Despite being King of Judah, Jehoshaphat clearly knew who was truly in charge. He was willing to concede that God was omnipotent, so he needed to regain trust in Him.

I look up to the mountains—does my help come from there? My help comes from the LORD, who made heaven and earth! He will not let you stumble; the one who watches over you will not slumber. Indeed, he who watches over Israel never slumbers or sleeps. (Psalm 121:1-4 - NLT).

It is better to take refuge in the LORD than to trust in people. (Psalm 118:8 - NLT).

The main objective of prayer is to address God and not be preoccupied with the enemy or his threats. What must feature in prayer is our ongoing dialogue with God. This is not the time to address any other being, no matter the pressures being felt or the challenges being experienced.

Jehoshaphat's action during a national crisis provides a clear-cut example of how godly leadership responds in the face of imminent enemy threats. Despite having a sizeable army of over a million strong, the opposition armies comprising the Moabites, Ammonites, and Mount Seir were far greater in number and were marching in their direction to wage war. This vast army was coming to confront Judah and represented the greatest security threat they had ever faced.

Being terrified by the news that he had received, Jehoshaphat saw as his only recourse a consultation with God. It is never the size of the problem that matters but the greatness of your God. Without question, the king believed that God was their first concern and not their last resort. There was no doubt in his mind that the sovereign God was able to deliver them.

Jehoshaphat, as the king of Judah, was going to make an impassioned plea for God's deliverance, being aware of God's omnipotence. The king reminded God of His past faithfulness, while expressing the people's helplessness and seeking divine intervention against this looming threat.

In lieu of the circumstances, he was terrified and sought God for divine guidance. The fear he felt did not cause him to run away or become paralysed but rather to repose trust and confidence in God. He knew that if you have time to pray, you still have time, making him proclaim a fast and prayer. This was a corporate gathering that brought together all Judah to Jerusalem. The nature of the threat required participation by all to seek God's intervention through corporate intercession.

Jehoshaphat was certainly unafraid to appear vulnerable to the people as they collectively sought God's intervention. He was unwilling to trust in human resources or agency but rather gave the entire situation over into the hands of God. He felt that his responsibility was to lead the nation in prayer to demonstrate their dependency on God and not themselves.

He speaks initially to God's supremacy and trustworthiness, which would inspire faith and confidence in Him and His ability. He was very sincere in his appraisal of God, having had a personal encounter with Him over the years, and he purposefully walked in the earlier example of his father. It was clear from Jehoshaphat's acknowledgment of God that he was in awe of him. How you approach God will reflect how He is viewed in your sight. Getting close to God should never silence or bring into question our reverence for Him. Jehoshaphat's prayer reveals that we must believe in God's plan and trust in His power. It is imperative that we have a knowledge of God's Word and hold on to the promises that He has made to us as the king did.

Jehoshaphat's prayer encourages all who serve God and are desirous of approaching Him in prayer, especially in times of adversity.

Acknowledging God's power - emphasizes God's sovereignty and power, recognizing that no one can stand against Him. God is indeed God over all the earth, and all power and might belong to Him. He is the ruler of—and the ruler over—all His creation. God definitely has power and control over circumstances that may seem insurmountable. The best way to navigate uncertainties is to trust the omniscient God. It is clear that the king was in awe and reverence regarding this God that he had come to know personally.

Remembered God's past deeds – Faith is rooted in the past, whilst hope looks to the future. The past acts of God become the template for trusting Him in the present and remaining expectant for the future. The acts of God speak volumes to His character and commitment to His people. The king was able to affirm in this prayer God's faithfulness in granting victory to His people in the past, which now became the basis for believing that it would continue as they remained resolute in trust. The king was confident that God was watching over them and would always be with them, so he could believe God for deliverance. The history of the nation clearly demonstrated God's unfailing mercies. This was not the prayer of someone with a mere acquaintance with God but one who knew Him personally and had walked with Him over the years.

Pleading God's promises – God's covenant relationship with His people had stood the test of time, and most certainly, the king believed would continue. There were crucial benefits that were attached to these covenants. The king was quick to embrace these promises believing that the provisions still held true. He was adamant that the people had a right to lay claim and that God would never stand aside to see the demise of a people He had invested so heavily in. This prayer was not to educate God but rather to reaffirm the people's commitment to Him, undergirded by their knowledge of His Word. Pleading God's promises was also an acknowledgment of his dependency on God.

Humbly depending on God – The king was quick to assert in prayer their limitations, but recognized God's strength and eternal might. In the face of the impending crisis, they did not have the solution, evidenced by the phrase, *"we are powerless before this vast number that comes to fight against us."* Greater reliance and trust are based on an acknowledgment of both weakness and inability, especially in the face of a crisis. Complete reliance on God rather than their own personal strengths is being advanced by this spiritual leader of the nation.

Not only was Jehoshaphat the political leader, but he was now in the face of the imminent threat. He was now providing spiritual oversight, showing how a godly nation deals with the threat of an imminent crisis. The hard questions that he posed required a response from God, and he was not disappointed. Remember, it is illegal to pray and not expect God to respond. In responding, God can either speak directly or indirectly. The response should be actively listening and responding to His instructions, which Jehoshaphat did.

Knowing God means knowing when He speaks and being submissive once we have heard. The message was to both the king and all Judah, outlining a divine strategy for victory. God chose not to utilize Jehoshaphat's army for victory but provided it by Himself. Their part was not to fear but to trust Him completely. They engaged in praise and worship after the prayer as they acknowledged the sovereignty of God in bringing the crisis to an expected end. Once again, it was proven that the power of prayer lies in the ability of a sovereign God. The king, having prayed, felt secure in the response that God had given and rejoiced with the people for divine intervention.

When all the surrounding kingdoms heard that the LORD himself had fought against the enemies of Israel, the fear of God came over them. So Jehoshaphat's kingdom was at peace, for his God had given him rest on every side. (2 Chronicles 20:29-30 - NLT).

Chapter Seven

Seek And You Shall Find

"Keep on asking, and you will receive what you ask for. Keep on seeking, and you will find. Keep on knocking, and the door will be opened to you. For everyone who asks, receives. Everyone who seeks, finds. And to everyone who knocks, the door will be opened." (Matthew 7:7-8 - NLT).

Embedded in these words of Jesus is the clarion call for intimacy. We are not searching for God because He is MIA (missing in action) or AWOL (absent without leave) but primarily because our hearts ache with an inner longing to be in His presence.

The seeking must begin with a desire for Him more than for what He can give. This must be carefully thought out and given priority attention. He will be found by those who seek Him. Before we even thought of it, His invitation was extended to us. We must now become committed to the overall process. Seeking is not a calendar event but an overall journey where we faithfully allow Him to be the guide. There must be no reluctance or inhibition on our part but a total yielding to the process.

The seeking of which the scripture espouses is a continuous affair; we never stop but simply continue as we are given unrestricted access. There is a measure to which God wants us to know and experience Him, so He continuously beckons. We voluntarily lay aside all fears and uncertainties as our journey to intimacy will not be fraught with hesitancy. The most crucial preparation needed for the overall process is a yielded or surrendered heart—one that is fully prepared and open to embrace Him. Sincerity in prayer will cause us to submit rather than resist His will.

We seek Him because we love Him more than anything else in our finite existence. It is a treasuring based on revelation that keeps pulling us forward and upward. God reveals but we seek based on His guidance. To be sure, God is already where we are endeavouring to reach.

In our seeking, we must twin revelation with patience. This is not a journey to be endured but rather one to enjoy and be ecstatic about. The heart can long for what it cannot fully explain but pursues with certainty. It is the desire to go to a destination you have never been to or experienced before, but you are certain that your arrival has been approved and that your efforts will be rewarded. Following God will cause you to stay the course and arrive at the intended destination.

But from there you will search again for the LORD your God. And if you search for him with all your heart and soul, you will find him. (Deuteronomy 4:29 - NLT).

Searching or seeking God would involve reading the scriptures, praying, and interacting with other believers in fellowship. These basic forms of fellowship must include listening and talking with each other. A general dislike of prayer or simply seeing it as a religious obligation can become a barrier to effective communication.

God's presence is not dependent on location, even though He may choose to reveal Himself at specific places. Your heart will always be the major place of His abode. God may be ignored or not acknowledged, but He can never be excluded from His creation. God is always there. Being sovereign, God cannot be barred from revealing Himself within the sphere of what He has created. His self-revelation does not require man's approval. God reveals His glory that He may receive glory.

I can never escape from your Spirit! I can never get away from your presence! If I go up to heaven, you are there; if I go down to the grave, you are there. If I ride the wings of the morning, if I dwell by the farthest oceans, even there your hand will guide me, and your strength will support me. I could ask the darkness to hide me and the light around me to become night but even in darkness I cannot hide from you. To you the night shines as bright as day. Darkness and light are the same to you. (Psalm 139:7-12 - NLT).

73

God has made Himself available so that the diligent will be able to find Him. It is the earnest and dedicated seeker whose efforts will be rewarded. We must exercise a conscious effort on our part to draw closer to God as we seek to align our beliefs with His. There is no greater and more fulfilling joy than simply being in His presence. It is definitely worth both the effort and the wait. The invisible God will be found by visible men who are in passionate pursuit of Him.

Chapter Eight

My Soul Follows Hard After You

I cling to you; your strong right hand holds me securely. (Psalm 63:8 - NLT).

It is all too easy to desire to engage God in prayer, but the thrust of our hearts is not going after Him. There can be words and no intimacy, but in our conversations with God, it must include words and heart combined to produce intimacy. Whenever there is a lack of sincerity, intimacy is compromised. Trusting God is based primarily on His integrity. He will always fulfil His promises concerning His people. Our expectation must always align itself with His Word, which cannot fail. Let us understand that it is more Him that holds us than us holding on to Him.

As the deer longs for streams of water, so I long for you, O God. I thirst for God, the living God. When can I go and stand before him? (Psalm 42:1-2 - NLT).

Our outer commitment to God must be fuelled by our inner desires for Him. The Psalmist expresses a deep, almost desperate, yearning for God, comparing the soul's thirst for God to a deer's thirst for water, emphasizing the vital need for a relationship with the living God. The desperation and intensity of this drive cannot be overlooked. God is absolutely needed for man's spiritual survival. The longing expressed by the Psalmist is both personal and intimate and underscores the point that separation from God was not an option. The personal distress and longing for God are here emphasised. The thirst experienced by the Psalmist becomes a powerful motivator and absolute priority in his quest for God.

It is time to consider what value we place in our moments of solitude with Him when we pause from the noise and the busyness to be both at one and at peace with Him.

May all my thoughts be pleasing to him, for I rejoice in the LORD. (Psalm 104:34 – NLT).

Intimacy speaks of intense preoccupation with the person of our admiration and devotion. The struggle with intimacy at times is that of perception versus reality. Without knowing God, it becomes brittle and fragmented. We can't know and not desire God. The knowledge of the holy brings enlightenment, understanding, and a deep sense of belonging.

May the words of my mouth and the meditation of my heart be pleasing to you, O LORD, my rock and my redeemer. (Psalm 19:14 - NLT).

76

Intimacy is about responding and ensuring that the deepest needs of others are met—the felt needs rather than the surface needs. Intimacy with God must therefore be seen as a bold partnership where finiteness and infiniteness meet.

My heart has heard you say, "Come and talk with me." And my heart responds, "LORD, I am coming." (Psalm 27:8 - NLT).

This is evidently a call that must not be ignored and an invitation that holds so much promise. Without knowing all the elements of what will be discussed, our hearts ache with expectancy and are indeed flooded with supreme joy. What an invitation and, correspondingly, what a God. He knows our inner longings and is able to furnish us with such immense and inexpressible joy.

The call resonates within the corridors of our minds and the very depth of our being. He calls, and we must respond, making this our priority and first port of call.

Like the fire on the altar, our desire for God should never diminish; we should always maintain a fervour and passion for Him. The more we have of God, the greater our desire for Him should be. Each interaction paves the way for the next. It should be like having a desire for the next meeting to commune even before the current one is over.

A "God chaser" refers to someone whose passion for God's presence drives them to relentlessly seek Him. The greatest reward for seeking God cannot simply be the acquisition of material things but, more so, experiencing His abiding presence.

Chapter Nine

Alone With God

That evening after sunset, many sick and demon-possessed people were brought to Jesus. The whole town gathered at the door to watch. So Jesus healed many people who were sick with various diseases, and he cast out many demons. But because the demons knew who he was, he did not allow them to speak. Before daybreak the next morning, Jesus got up and went out to an isolated place to pray. (Mark 1:32-35 - NLT).

The real secret to the miraculous displays of God's power among His people was inextricably linked to the intimate moments that preceded and succeeded each mission attempt. Intimacy with God was always central to these power surge displays. Jesus adopted a model of rising early before others to spend time unequivocally with God. These private moments were personal and prolonged.

No other relationships were as significant, and all seemed to revolve around the centrality of the God moments. If you miss God in private, the public authority will suffer. Public ministry must never interfere with private moments with God. The one must complement the other.

Intimacy with God must become a habit rather than a diversion or digression from the essentials of life. Real life always begins with intimate moments. These moments can be both planned or unplanned, but there must be the discipline and the passion to carry them out.

There is a direct relationship between the frequency of prayer and the depth of our love relationship with God; neither stands alone. The one requires the other.

May all my thoughts be pleasing to him, for I rejoice in the LORD. (Psalm 104:34 - NLT).

Our greatest preoccupation must be about God and the direct influence of His Word and presence on our lives. Our thoughts should always spill over into our intimate conversations with God.

Let us be aware that solitude geared towards intimacy is not being anti-social. We cannot and must never allow our existing relationship to take precedence over what we share with God. In fact, we hide nothing but feel free to disclose every facet of our lives to Him without fear.

I will bless the LORD who guides me; even at night my heart instructs me. I know the LORD is always with me. I will not be shaken, for he is right beside me. No wonder my heart is glad, and I rejoice. My body rests in safety. (Psalm 16:7-9 - NLT).

The silence in the solitude gives us time to be with God void of all distractions. Those things that would normally compete or vie for our attention have been stripped of their ability. Intimacy requires focus, which this alone time affords.

Spending time alone with God fosters a deeper, more personal relationship, allowing for quiet reflection, prayer, and hearing His voice, ultimately leading to spiritual growth and a stronger connection with Him. We are never lonely when we are alone with God. The exposure is edifying and brings a sense of us being centred around the priority of life, which is being with God.

Spending time alone with God allows for reflection, self-examination, and a renewed focus on spiritual values, leading to personal growth and a stronger relationship with Him. In this atmosphere, it becomes easier to discern His will as we repose trust and confidence in His guidance and direction. Then comes clarity and an overwhelming sense of purpose as we navigate the upper reaches of intimacy.

Chapter Ten

When You Pray

Once Jesus was in a certain place praying. As he finished, one of his disciples came to him and said, "Lord, teach us to pray, just as John taught his disciples." Jesus said, "This is how you should pray: "Father, may your name be kept holy. May your Kingdom come soon. Give us each day the food we need, and forgive us our sins, as we forgive those who sin against us. And don't let us yield to temptation." (Luke 11:1-4 - NLT).

Not only did the disciples observe Jesus and John's disciples' prayer, but they also desired to have that direct communion and communication with God themselves. Intimacy is based on direct and not indirect association. Jesus pointed out that prayer is highly relational, and speaks to a direct familial tie between us and God. We are all His children and have both the access to Him and the right to call Him Father.

Intimacy in prayer is bold, enabling, and empowering. Prayer is never the time to cower in fear but to approach God respectfully and reverentially. It is important to pray according to knowledge, ideally from an informed position. Rest assured that prayer is an invention of God, and if anyone should know the depths of it, Jesus would. The model prayer He gave taught the principles concerning how to engage with God in this most intimate of the spiritual disciplines.

Jesus quickly acceded to the request of the disciples with the full knowledge that prayer is not optional or discretionary; it is imperative. It is not "if you pray" but "when you pray." While Jesus was seen by the disciples praying, it is not a public spectacle where prayer is offered so that we may be recognised by men to be persons of prayer.

Prayerful intimacy will contain the elements of transparency and trust. Jesus, as was His practice, would seek a place of solitude away from the hustle and bustle of ministry activities to be alone with God. The disciples recognised the weight of importance that Jesus attached to these moments and wanted to emulate Him and walk in that level of fellowship that He displayed with God.

Through prayer, God endears Himself to all who will approach Him in sincerity and truth. Reverence and respect are the twin pillars on which intimacy with God is built.

So let us come boldly to the throne of our gracious God. There we will receive his mercy, and we will find grace to help us when we need it most. (Hebrews 4:16 - NLT).

Prayer is a God-initiative that demands a response from man. We come not because we may but because we must. The most important invitation a human being can ever receive is that of communing with your Creator, God. Prayer is not just a good idea; it is a God-idea. Prayer is not for the celebrated few but for all. We have equal access to God through Jesus Christ our Lord. When we come to pray, we must recognize that the audience is one. Therefore, we do not pray to impress others but to connect with God.

An important aspect of praying reverentially is that it requires us to spend quality time with our Creator. It should not be rushed and hurried; there should definitely be moments for conscious reflection and effective listening. Intimacy is built through time and patience. It takes time to be known and understood. Prayer gives us a distinct opportunity to be heard and to be guided because of the two-way level of interaction. God is as devoted to listening to His children as He is to responding. Remember that in prayer, we may not get what we want but what we need. We continue to trust God and accept the outcome He gives.

In prayer, we acknowledge that God is the head of our lives, our families, and His church and that He has not abdicated His responsibility of overseeing the world. God supplies, sustains, and comforts us with the realization that there is nothing too hard for Him to do.

We approach God, fully aware that His will must be done on earth as it is already done in heaven. The manifestation of

God's kingdom here on earth is indicative of His right to rule.

While we utilize prayer points, we must never forget the point of prayer. True intimacy in prayer will always have as its outcome honouring God. No one can ever be as important as Him. God is our number one priority at all levels of our relationships.

We pray with confidence because intimacy in prayer requires us to be loosed from the bondages of insecurity. The fear factor is never accommodated in our moments when we are seeking God. Our prayers therefore are never motivated by selfishness or self-centeredness. Our prayers are always focused on God and the fulfillment of His will.

A major part of our considerations in prayer is that access to God is not dependent on geographic location or ethnicity. He is the God of all people. Consistent prayer is going to require discipline and tenacity. We communicate frequently with God because we love the intimate relationship that we share.

You can pray and not love, but you can't love God and not pray. The primary motivation for prayer is love. Prayer to the believer should be both normal and natural. It is quite in order for there to be introspection before expression. This is not taking away from the spontaneity of prayer. Unplanned occasions where, despite the location, we are overwhelmed by a desire to communicate with our Father is thoroughly embraced and accepted by Him. We, however, concretize our desire for an in-depth interchange with Him where time is not a major concern. After having experienced God, the soul will never be satisfied with anything less.

Chapter Eleven

The Tabernacle and Intimacy

It was Moses' practice to take the Tent of Meeting and set it up some distance from the camp. Everyone who wanted to make a request of the LORD would go to the Tent of Meeting outside the camp. Whenever Moses went out to the Tent of Meeting, all the people would get up and stand in the entrances of their own tents. They would all watch Moses until he disappeared inside. As he went into the tent, the pillar of cloud would come down and hover at its entrance while the LORD spoke with Moses. When the people saw the cloud standing at the entrance of the tent, they would stand and bow down in front of their own tents. Inside the Tent of Meeting, the LORD would speak to Moses face to face, as one speaks to a friend. Afterward Moses would return to the camp, but the young man who assisted him, Joshua son of Nun, would remain behind in the Tent of Meeting. (Exodus 33:7-11 - NLT).

In the Bible, the tabernacle symbolizes a close and intimate relationship with God. This portable, temporary temple vividly portrayed what a deep-seated connection with God was all about. The tabernacle was a physical representation of the spiritual process that God created to ensure that man would get close to and dwell with Him. This portable sanctuary symbolizes God's desire to dwell among His people and provide a place for intimate encounters with Himself. This was a place of accessibility where divinity met with humanity. God desires closeness and fellowship, all of which are available through the tabernacle. Thus, man could approach God exactly as dictated by Him.

The basic divisions of the tabernacle and its various implements model for us the importance of prayer and its goal, which is intimacy with God. The tabernacle was meant to be with them along the journey, and so it is that prayer is the mainstay of the believer and is an important focal point that connects us with God.

The tabernacle was a place for frequent and meaningful encounters between Moses and God. It was said that God spoke to him face to face. This was a clear depiction of the type of relationship that God desired with man, one in which there could be constant and open communication with Him. The fact that the tabernacle was mobile signified that God wanted man to have an experience with Him every step of the way in life.

The tabernacle was a place for crucial encounters where God would provide guidance, and the people could experience His presence. God desired to be known and experienced not as a distant deity but as a loving and ever-present God. The theophany of a cloud that covered the tabernacle was a visible sign of the invisible God's power and presence.

The very design of the tabernacle was meant to foster an intimate relationship between God and the people and was built based on trust and obedience. It also symbolized God's holiness and the need to approach Him with reverence and love. The intimate relationship that God desires with us is mutually exclusive. Our desire to be intimate with Him will exclude and demarcate other relationships as not being on the same level. The tabernacle was not just a place for God to dwell but a place of worship based on relationship. It was there that one could, in awe, enjoy the richness associated with the presence of God. Being with God and hearing Him speak is an experience that we must be in unrelenting pursuit of. Nothing in this world is as important and urgent as being in His presence and acknowledging His will with the view of being completely obedient.

The tabernacle was a visible place for prayerful encounters. God will never entrust the true riches of His presence to prayerless people.

The Old Testament paints a vivid picture of intimacy for us in the image of the tabernacle, the ancient Jew's centre for worship. When God gave Moses directions for building the tabernacle, it included three main areas: firstly, the "outer court"; secondly, "the inner court"; and thirdly, "the holiest of all" or the "holy of holies." These areas represented stages through which a worshiper would pass as he drew closer to God.

The "outer court" was the courtyard. In this public place, people mingled, talked, and prepared to take deeper steps into the places of worship. This was the most familiar part of the tabernacle to most people.

The "inner court" was the place where the worshiper would meet a priest, confess their sins, and offer a suitable sacrifice for their sins. It was the point that connected the dwelling place of the people ("outer court") with the dwelling place of God ("holiest of all").

The "holiest of all" was the place where the glory of God dwelt. His presence was there. One could not get any closer to the heart of God than in this sacred room. And, yet, it was such a holy place that an unauthorized individual who rushed into it would be struck dead. No, careful preparation had to be made by the high priest to enter that holy place, and he could only enter it once a year.

The tabernacle is a guide for our prayer life:

- *The Gate (Jesus)* – In the same way that the gate is the entrance to the tabernacle, so we come to God the Father through our Lord Jesus Christ.

- *The Outer Court (Repentance and cleansing)* – This contained the brazen altar and laver speaking to repentance and cleansing. As we approach God with humility and confess our sins, then we are cleansed by the blood of Jesus.

- *The Holy Place (Praise and Intercession)* – This contained the lampstand and table of shrew bread, symbolic of the presence of God and the need for His light and guidance. We should earnestly seek God's wisdom and guidance in our lives as we come with thanksgiving and praise.

- *The Holy of Holies (God's Presence)* – This is where the Ark of the Covenant rested—it being the place of God's presence and the ultimate focus of our worship. As we draw close to God in prayer, we begin to know Him and experience His glory.

- *The Priestly Garment* – This teaches us that we do not come before God in our own righteousness but by the righteousness of Jesus Christ through faith. Salvation is a necessary pre-requisite for us to radiate the glory of Jesus and pray effectively.

The very life of God in Christ is here modeled by the tabernacle, pointedly speaking to God's desire to dwell among His people.

The furniture within the tabernacle had tremendous significance. The tabernacle furniture, as described in the Old Testament, included the Ark of the Covenant, the Table of Shewbread, the Golden Lampstand, the Altar of Incense, the Bronze Basin, and the Altar of Burnt Offering.

The Ark of the Covenant

Many things can be said about the Ark of the Covenant, including that it is symbolic of God's presence. The ark, a sacred chest containing the Ten Commandments, symbolized God's presence and covenant with His people, with the mercy seat (covering the ark) representing God's grace and forgiveness.

The Table of Shewbread

This symbolized God as the bread of life. He is the only one who can satisfy the spiritual hunger of the soul. God provides and cares for us, knowing exactly what we need. Life should never be lived apart from God's provision and presence. Jesus is referred to as the bread that came down from heaven to satisfy the longing of the soul. God is also capable of meeting the physical needs of humanity.

The Golden Lampstand

This symbolized God as the light of the world, showing people how to approach and worship. Jesus Christ came into the world to give light and illumination so that we might know and serve God, thus symbolizing the lampstand. The lampstand also symbolizes the believers, God's people, as the light of the world. It also represents the Word of God, which enables a person to know and serve God.

The Altar of Incense

This is the symbol of the prayers and communion of God's people ascending to God. This taught that Christ, our great High Priest, is always praying and living in an unbroken communion with God the Father, interceding for God's people. We need to pray without ceasing and develop an unbroken communion with God.

The Bronze Basin (laver)

Used for ritual purification, where the priests washed their hands and feet before entering the tent or approaching the altar. This speaks to the cleansing necessary before offering service to God. It is Jesus who has the power to wash and cleanse us from all sin; thus, the believer needs to be on guard to avoid being entangled by sin.

The Altar of Burnt Offering

This symbolized the need for atonement, for reconciliation with God. This was where God met with His people who needed atonement for sins. This speaks to God's ability to deliver His people through all the trials and temptations of life.

The Furniture of the Tabernacle

Ark of the Covenant
(Ex. 25:10-22)
The ark was most sacred of all the furniture in the tabernacle. Here the Hebrews kept a copy of the Ten Commandments, which summarized the whole covenant.

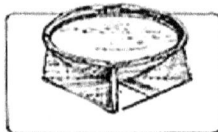

Bronze Laver
(Ex. 30:17-21)
It was to the laver of bronze that the priests would come for cleansing. They must be pure to enter the presence of God.

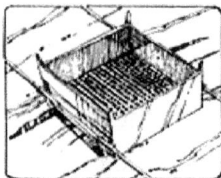

Altar of Burnt Offering
(Ex. 27:1-8)
Animal sacrifices were offered on this altar, located in the court in front of the tabernacle. The blood of the sacrifice was sprinkled on the four horns of the altar.

Golden Lampstand
(Ex. 25:31-40)
The gold lampstand stood in the holy place, opposite the table of showbread. It held seven lamps, flat bowls in which a wick lay with one end in the oil of the bowl and the lighted end hanging out.

Table of Showbread
(Ex. 25:23-30)
The table of showbread was a stand on which the offerings were placed. Always in God's presence on the table were the 12 loaves of bread representing the 12 tribes.

Altar of Incense
(Ex. 30:1-10)
The altar of incense inside the tabernacle was much smaller than the altar of burnt offering outside. The incense burned on the altar was a perfume of a sweet-smelling aroma.

The tabernacle signified a place where God and man could meet and intimate communication could be effected. In Jesus, God and man unite.

Chapter Twelve

Fervent Effectual Prayer

Confess your sins to each other and pray for each other so that you may be healed. The earnest prayer of a righteous person has great power and produces wonderful results. Elijah was as human as we are, and yet when he prayed earnestly that no rain would fall, none fell for three and a half years! Then, when he prayed again, the sky sent down rain and the earth began to yield its crops. (James 5:16-18 - NLT).

The type of praying that engages God will always be effective in producing results. Prayers are not deemed powerful because of who prays but because of the God who answers. The power to provide an answer lies in God and not us. God allows us to partner with Him, so as we are guided by the Holy Spirit, we pray but the response is left entirely up to Him.

In all matters of prayer, it is important for us to understand our dependency and God's sovereignty. It is He who ultimately decides how He will respond, and we submit to

His will being done on the earth. Prayer was never meant to be a tool of manipulation or coercion but rather one of awareness, revelation, and submission. Prayer reveals God's all-sufficiency and our dependency. We must trust God relating to the outcome of all our prayers. God can cause our private prayers to yield public results. For every man who commits himself to prayer, there is a God who will commit to answer.

And we are confident that he hears us whenever we ask for anything that pleases him. And since we know he hears us when we make our requests, we also know that he will give us what we ask for. (1 John 5:14-15 - NLT).

It is God who sets the parameters for our prayers. It is imperative therefore that the objective of our prayers is in alignment with His. The effectiveness of our passionate and sincere prayers is wholly dependent on the response of God. It is true that sometimes we pray for what we want, but God supplies what we need. Even though prayer is a biblical imperative, God still encourages believers to be consistent in praying. God has more answers than problems we have committed to Him in prayer. The real problem of the age is not unanswered prayers but unoffered prayers.

God's will moves Him to an action-oriented response, which is why it becomes necessary to pray from an informed position. Praying in ignorance is not a virtue, and neither is it encouraged. To pray God's will, we must know it. The scriptures clearly reveal His will, and prayer will provide revelation that reveals His will. When we pray the scriptures, we are assured that He will stand by His Word to ensure that the promises contained come to pass.

Don't act thoughtlessly, but understand what the Lord wants you to do. (Ephesians 5:17 - NLT).

Once we understand what God's will is, we can approach Him with much confidence and certainty in the partnership of prayer. His will is the ultimate guarantee that the outcome has already been determined. We therefore move from selfish to selfless prayers as His will becomes our prayer points and our main priority. God is a God of performance. He is faithful to execute what He has spoken about.

Praying fervently is not just limited to passion but must embrace the following features. We must pray with a sincere heart as we seek to connect and embrace God. It is always too early to give up on God in prayer; thus, we must persist or persevere. To cement it all, we are praying according to how we have been authorized, for our prayer is consistent with the demands of the Word. We must also encourage the confession of sins as we pray one for another to mitigate against hindrances to effective praying. Thus, right heart, attitude, and strong commitment to God and His Word are essential parameters. God is the one who guarantees the results of this type of prayer.

We can speak and pray with confidence when our prayers are aligned with His will. Examples of fervent and effectual prayer in the Bible include Hannah's passionate plea for a son, Elijah's persistent prayer for rain, and Daniel's heartfelt confession and supplication. In 1 Kings 18, Elijah, a prophet known for his boldness, prays fervently for rain after a long drought. He sends his servant to look for signs of rain seven times, and only after the seventh time does the servant report a small cloud rising from the sea. The rain comes, and the drought is broken.

The passage in James 5 is very instructive and informative. Those who are suffering, their first recourse should be to submit the situation in its entirety to God. For the sick, the elders of the church should be summoned, and they should intercede on their behalf, anointing them with oil as a symbol of the power and presence of the Holy Spirit in action. Praying in faith means with humble confidence that God will heal. God can reveal for each specific situation what His will is. We, however, must confidently leave all such matters into His capable hands and trust Him to do what He deems fit. The prayer of faith is not prayed out of concern for God's reputation if there is no healing. We understand that God is sovereign and omnipotent in all His ways, and He casts the deciding vote.

It is not our greatness that moves God but His will. The passage clearly cites that Elijah was a man with a nature like ours. The Bible uses him as a model of earnest prayer, signifying that his heart was in tune with what God desired. What he prayed for was clearly what God wanted to accomplish. Like Elijah, may we have the heart of God as we engage in earnest praying.

The outcome that Elijah prayed for was based on what God wanted to be done. The fervency or forcefulness applies to the outcome of the prayer, not the earnestness of the prayer: it is God who determines which prayers are answered.

Chapter Thirteen

God's Love Revealed Through Prayer

Long ago the LORD said to Israel: "I have loved you, my people, with an everlasting love. With unfailing love I have drawn you to myself." (Jeremiah 31:3 - NLT).

God will respond, even before we formulate our prayers in words because He knows the end from the beginning. Creating an avenue or an outlet for us to communicate with Him is indeed a distinct measure of His love for all humanity. He is consistently clear that the repentant soul will have unparalleled access to the riches of His grace.

Despite the great patriarchs of the faith and the monumental work they were inspired to do, God still desires a personal connection with all who will take this walk of faith with Him. The communication with us that resonates with Him is done on an intimate plane. He wants both your hand and your heart.

God desires for us to know His will so that we will pray consistently with that in mind so He would reward us with answers.

I will answer them before they even call to me. While they are still talking about their needs, I will go ahead and answer their prayers! (Isaiah 65:24 - NLT).

Uncommon access to God requires Him to share with us His wisdom concerning what is appropriate for the situation at hand. God always listens, and He cares deeply about His people. He provides peace, comfort, and guidance, especially in challenging times.

God, by way of His Holy Spirit, allows us to feel that closeness to Him and the awareness that even when we don't understand, He is working on our behalf. The highest expression of God's love for humanity is reflected in the sacrificial atoning death of Jesus on the cross of Calvary. This procured for us eternal redemption and unlimited access to God through His son, Jesus Christ.

We can experience God's love through prayer, which is a powerful tool for intimacy. Prayer allows for a deeper connection and revelation of God and His character. Our active pursuit and seeking after God is an indication of how much we love and desire Him.

When I think of all this, I fall to my knees and pray to the Father, the Creator of everything in heaven and on earth. I pray that from his glorious, unlimited resources he will empower you with inner strength through his Spirit. Then Christ will make his home in your hearts as you trust in him. Your roots will grow down into God's love and keep you strong. And may you have the power to understand, as all God's people should, how wide, how long, how high, and how deep his love is. May you experience the love of Christ, though it is too great to understand fully. Then you will be made complete with all the fullness of life and power that comes from God. (Ephesians 3:14-19 - NLT).

Paul prays for the Ephesians, seeking God's grace to strengthen them spiritually, enabling them to comprehend the vastness of Christ's love and to be filled with God's fullness. The facility of prayer is one of the clearest indications of God's love in that He is giving us access to Himself. The depth of this love can only be comprehended as He reveals that to us through our prayerful considerations with Him.

It is Jesus in our hearts who gives us the capacity to experience and demonstrate God's love. When we understand what salvation has wrought on our behalf, we see an active demonstration of God's love through Christ. The more we pray, the greater our capacity to receive and acknowledge the depth of His love.

God's desire for intimacy with man must be understood as a testimony of the love He desires for us to share in communion and fellowship with Him. Sincere praying will evoke a heart of gratitude towards God as we are comforted by His love that surrounds us.

We are capable of loving God because of how He has extravagantly bestowed His love upon us. This love is enriching and rewarding, the depth of which is only unveiled to those who share a vital relationship with Him. As Paul did, so do we vocalise our acknowledgment of His love that eclipses all that man can provide.

We are confident of God's indwelling presence and are never apprehensive of divine love. The internal witness of God's abiding Spirit brings the truth and witnesses to our spirit concerning the vastness of God's love. God not only listens to us but He speaks to build us up within and provide us with hope and security concerning future outcomes. What we have experienced through Christ takes the Spirit of God to give us a modicum of understanding as we pray what really has been wrought. This is incomprehensible to mortal man and can only be measured by the Spirit who is at work within us. What cannot be understood through natural sight is experienced through revelation.

We all need this spiritual inner sensitivity in dealing with matters of the Spirit as they are communicated to us. The Holy Spirit will prepare our inner being to acknowledge and truly grasp the nature of God's love for us. The Spirit of God will guide us into the truth of God's love toward us as we give Him leverage to pray through us but also to give us understanding.

Well then, what shall I do? I will pray in the spirit, and I will also pray in words I understand. I will sing in the spirit, and I will also sing in words I understand. (1 Corinthians 14:15 - NLT).

When the Spirit of truth comes, he will guide you into all truth. He will not speak on his own but will tell you what he has heard. He will tell you about the future. He will bring me glory by telling you whatever he receives from me. All that belongs to the Father is mine; this is why I said, 'The Spirit will tell you whatever he receives from me.' (John 16:13-15 - NLT).

The measure of love we receive will be in direct proportion to our yielding to the Holy Spirit as He channels the prayer through us. We will know and experience simultaneously as we submit to His leading in prayer.

This prayerful experience is a journey we undertake that will require time and patience. We submit to the nudging of the Holy Spirit, but we work with His pace. After all, prayer is the great and glorious adventure that takes us into the deepest realms of God's love.

There is the understanding through prayer that we are being afforded God's best for our lives. This will cause our level of gratitude and expression of love to rise in soulful praise to Him. We grow in our love for God through prayer by always making Him the centre of our lives and all our decision-making. We also grow in our love for God by active listening with the intention of submitting and following in obedience. This now makes it easier to shift our love of self to loving and obeying God.

If you love me, obey my commandments. (John 14:15 – NLT).

Prayer is a radical act and expression of our love for God. Jesus prayed for us, so we, by extension, will pray for others. Through prayer, God heals and restores us from having been ravaged by this broken world.

Jesus' prayer on the cross is a direct revelation of the tremendous nature of God's love for humanity. Prayer is an intimate invitation to connect with God.

When they came to a place called The Skull, they nailed him to the cross. And the criminals were also crucified—one on his right and one on his left. Jesus said, "Father, forgive them, for they don't know what they are doing." And the soldiers gambled for his clothes by throwing dice. (Luke 23:33-34 - NLT),

Chapter Fourteen

The Secret of the Lord

"Should I hide my plan from Abraham?" the LORD asked. "For Abraham will certainly become a great and mighty nation, and all the nations of the earth will be blessed through him. I have singled him out so that he will direct his sons and their families to keep the way of the LORD by doing what is right and just. Then I will do for Abraham all that I have promised." (Genesis 18:17-19 - NLT).

The LORD is a friend to those who fear him. He teaches them his covenant. My eyes are always on the LORD, for he rescues me from the traps of my enemies. (Psalm 25:14-15 - NLT).

Abraham exhibited a quality that needs to be patterned by the current-day believing community. This has to do with a consistent and ongoing dialogue with God. This, in essence, is the basis of what we call prayer. God has set an irrevocable requirement that if we call, He will respond. He is not averse to spending quality time interacting with His sons and daughters. The invitation to meet with and talk with Him has been extended, and we need to, like Abraham, take full advantage of it.

God values and places a high premium on the relationship shared with Him. He will initiate a conversation whenever He deems it fit to both inform and make us aware of the important things in life. At these moments, we become acutely conscious of both His will and ways.

God, being sovereign, could have exercised His authority without making Abraham aware of His intentions toward Sodom. The intimate bond between the two resulted in God's willingness to share His imminent plans with Abraham. God's disclosure to Abraham was continent on the depth of the relationship they shared. Abraham's trust and reliance on God, who had called him out of an idolatrous culture, seemed sufficient for God to share with and entertain a discussion with Abraham concerning the future of the twin cities of Sodom and Gomorrah. God will share His secrets with those who share a deep relationship with Him. In fact, it is His divine prerogative to do so.

God's intimate counsel and wisdom are revealed, especially to those who have a covenant relationship with Him. This is not just knowing about but knowing God with the totality of our being. We know God through prayer and His intimate disclosures. It is evident that Abraham had a deep respect for God and served Him wholeheartedly. This caused God to make Abraham privy to the intricacies of His decision-making. He would not hide from Abraham what His

110

intended plans were but shared them with Him openly. There is indeed a direct correlation between intimacy and friendship.

The LORD is a friend to those who fear him. He teaches them his covenant. (Psalm 25:14 - NLT).

Abraham argued with God as a man would with a friend when God's intention was made clear to him. The dialogue that ensued carries with it the idea of intercession, with Abraham playing a mediatorial role. God was willing to allow Abraham to share his heart before He responded.

And so it happened just as the Scriptures say: "Abraham believed God, and God counted him as righteous because of his faith." He was even called the friend of God. (James 2:23 - NLT).

Abraham was called a friend of God because of his strong faith and obedience to God. This relationship or bond was characterised by intimacy and understanding. They both listened and spoke with each other with integrity and transparency. Abraham's relationship with God had stood the test of time, and a notable feature of it was their constant communication with each other. Even through difficult and uncomfortable times, Abraham's commitment did not waver. He knew that genuine friendship could only thrive on honesty, love, and commitment to each other. Abraham's love for God was exemplified by his obedience and sacrifice. He believed what God said and held on to the promises with tenacity and hope. He knew that God would come through, and so was always supportive of God's agenda.

Abraham's friendship with God was further strengthened and undergirded by God's everlasting covenant and Abraham's faith in receiving and embracing the promises recorded in the divine agreement. When God called out to him, he responded affirmatively and subsequently moved into action.

The LORD had said to Abram, "Leave your native country, your relatives, and your father's family, and go to the land that I will show you. I will make you into a great nation. I will bless you and make you famous, and you will be a blessing to others. I will bless those who bless you and curse those who treat you with contempt. All the families on earth will be blessed through you." So Abram departed as the LORD had instructed, and Lot went with him. Abram was seventy-five years old when he left Haran. He took his wife, Sarai, his nephew Lot, and all his wealth—his livestock and all the people he had taken into his household at Haran— and headed for the land of Canaan. (Genesis 12:1-5 - NLT).

Believers under the new covenant are referred to as Abraham's seed; thus, the mutual association with God continues. Jesus reaffirmed this friendship that we as believers share with God, which is contingent upon adherence to certain requirements. Jesus' promise is abundantly clear that He will confide in those who meet the special conditions of friendship. We can celebrate the fact that we have unlimited access and communication with the Father, through our Lord and Saviour Jesus Christ. Honest, straightforward, and open communication is what characterises our friendship with God. Rest assured that God is not intimidated or thinks it inappropriate if we vent. What He desires is for us to bare our hearts so that communication can be achieved at the deepest level.

This is my commandment: Love each other in the same way I have loved you. There is no greater love than to lay down one's life for one's friends. You are my friends if you do what I command. I no longer call you slaves, because a master doesn't confide in his slaves. Now you are my friends, since I have told you everything the Father told me. (John 15:12-15 - NLT).

Chapter Fifteen

Adversary Versus Advocate

My dear children, I am writing this to you so that you will not sin. But if anyone does sin, we have an advocate who pleads our case before the Father. He is Jesus Christ, the one who is truly righteous. (1 John 2:1 - NLT).

Stay alert! Watch out for your great enemy, the devil. He prowls around like a roaring lion, looking for someone to devour. (1 Peter 5:8 - NLT).

Through prayer, our relationship status has been restored, and the Word of God declares us to be God's children. We have a unique and shared privilege that Jesus is pleading consistently on our behalf.

But to all who believed him and accepted him, he gave the right to become children of God. (John 1:12 - NLT).

Who then will condemn us? No one—for Christ Jesus died for us and was raised to life for us, and he is sitting in the place of honor at God's right hand, pleading for us. (Romans 8:34 - NLT).

We are extremely mindful concerning the existence and the potential threat of our adversary, the devil. We are however confident and reassured that God will take care of us. He values us and the relationship we share with Him too much to allow the enemy to destroy us.

So humble yourselves before God. Resist the devil, and he will flee from you. Come close to God, and God will come close to you. Wash your hands, you sinners; purify your hearts, for your loyalty is divided between God and the world. (James 4:7-8 - NLT).

Despite the sometimes-heinous nature of our backgrounds, having missed the mark or hit the wrong target, Jesus is still pleading for mercy on our behalf and extending grace to help us in times of need.

So let us come boldly to the throne of our gracious God. There we will receive his mercy, and we will find grace to help us when we need it most. (Hebrews 4:16 - NLT).

My dear children, I am writing this to you so that you will not sin. But if anyone does sin, we have an advocate who pleads our case before the Father. He is Jesus Christ, the one who is truly righteous. He himself is the sacrifice that atones for our sins—and not only our sins but the sins of all the world. (1 John 2:1-2 - NLT).

Answered prayer is the reassurance of God's love and compassion for us. It demonstrates how attentive God is to our every need, from the basic to the most challenging of them. As our advocate, Jesus argues the case on our behalf before God. He lives forever to make intercession for the saints according to God's will. He can be trusted to always rise to our defense.

The provision of peace and comfort amid the most challenging of circumstances speaks to the power of an intimate connection with God, building understanding geared towards more effective communication and communion and fostering the development of a healthy relationship between us and Him.

Through prayer, we receive instructions and are taught God's ways.

It is imperative and indeed important that prayer be a refreshing, renewing, intimate, and vital part of our Christian experience and exposure to God. It should never be relegated to the frustrating, mundane, obligatory, and disappointment of human interactions. Seeking to know God through prayer should be the most exhilarating, reverential, all-embracing, and loving interaction that we could have in this human existence. It should never deplete but complete us. Truly, without Him, we are nothing.

Chapter Sixteen

The Mystery of Intimacy

As the Scriptures say, "A man leaves his father and mother and is joined to his wife, and the two are united into one." This is a great mystery, but it is an illustration of the way Christ and the church are one. So again I say, each man must love his wife as he loves himself, and the wife must respect her husband. (Ephesians 5:31-33 - NLT).

Marriage is under siege by the enemy because marriage was created by God, and marriage is a picture of Christ's relationship to the church. Marriage is not just a good idea; it is a God-idea. The mystery of intimacy truly lies in its nature and symbolism. The unity between a wife and husband is representative of what must be shared by all who are in union with Christ. Human marriage is indeed the earthly image of God's divine plan. This is a unique metaphor that draws on God's supernatural intent of the two becoming one. The twin bonds of love and respect are crucial for this union to have permanence in the union of marriage.

Do not deprive each other of sexual relations, unless you both agree to refrain from sexual intimacy for a limited time so you can give yourselves more completely to prayer. Afterward, you should come together again so that Satan won't be able to tempt you because of your lack of self-control. (1 Corinthians 7:5 - NLT).

This passage clearly demonstrates the superiority of spiritual intimacy over sexual intimacy. This is the only occasion where permission is granted to a married couple to refrain that they both may devote time and space to deepen their spiritual walk and intimate relationship with God. No other forms of intimacy are ever allowed to compete with that which God requires of His people.

Spiritual intimacy is God-honouring and requires a disciplined approach by mutual consent for those who are married. Marriage should never affect our spiritual intimacy with God.

The purpose of temporary abstinence is often to allow for a period of focused prayer and spiritual reflection or for other reasons that both partners agree upon. Paul warns that withholding sexual intimacy can lead to temptation and potential immorality, emphasizing the importance of fulfilling marital needs and desires.

There should be no withholding of intimacy relating to our relationship with God, which is even more vital for our spiritual existence. It is a major injustice to be inconsistent regarding time spent with God because other things are considered more pressing.

Loving God first is not a competition with loving your spouse but rather a foundation for a better marriage. God comes first in all relationships, whether individually or as a couple. Evidently, the most significant relationship in life should be that intimate bond between man and God. To follow Jesus with your whole heart will require that He becomes primary and foremost in life.

"If you want to be my disciple, you must, by comparison, hate everyone else—your father and mother, wife and children, brothers and sisters—yes, even your own life. Otherwise, you cannot be my disciple. (Luke 14:26 - NLT).

The concept of oneness is at the heart of intimacy. What is shared between humans in no way compares to the level of intimacy that is shared with God. However, God is inviting us to a level of communion with Him that should never be ignored but accessed with all humility and love.

I pray that they will all be one, just as you and I are one— as you are in me, Father, and I am in you. And may they be in us so that the world will believe you sent me. "I have given them the glory you gave me, so they may be one as we are one. I am in them and you are in me. May they experience such perfect unity that the world will know that you sent me and that you love them as much as you love me." (John 17:21-23 - NLT).

Man was built and wired for different levels of intimacy, from the spiritual to the physical. Physical intimacy can never replace the highest level of intimacy, which is spiritual intimacy between man and his maker. Intimacy in marriage was never intended to replace intimacy with God. The physical intimacy between a man and a woman was designed to reflect the nature of true intimacy required by God the Father.

Then the LORD God said, "It is not good for the man to be alone. I will make a helper who is just right for him." (Genesis 2:18 - NLT).

God, in His eternal wisdom, recognised man's need for physical intimacy with his kind and created the perfect mate called woman for him. In the same way that a man is expected to leave father and mother to cleave to wife, we should abandon the world and its pleasures to cleave to God.

He gave names to all the livestock, all the birds of the sky, and all the wild animals. But still there was no helper just right for him. So the LORD God caused the man to fall into a deep sleep. While the man slept, the LORD God took out one of the man's ribs and closed up the opening. Then the LORD God made a woman from the rib, and he brought her to the man. "At last!" the man exclaimed. "This one is bone from my bone, and flesh from my flesh! She will be called 'woman,' because she was taken from 'man.'" This explains why a man leaves his father and mother and is joined to his wife, and the two are united into one. (Genesis 2:20-24 - NLT).

Marriage was never meant to disconnect man from God but rather to reconnect the couple in Him. The union of intimacy provides for two to become one, and two in God also become one. There is a subtle difference between being one in the flesh and one in the spirit.

Don't you realize that your bodies are actually parts of Christ? Should a man take his body, which is part of Christ, and join it to a prostitute? Never! And don't you realize that if a man joins himself to a prostitute, he becomes one body with her? For the Scriptures say, "The two are united into one." But the person who is joined to the Lord is one spirit with him. (1 Corinthians 6:15-17 - NLT).

As the Scriptures say, "A man leaves his father and mother and is joined to his wife, and the two are united into one." This is a great mystery, but it is an illustration of the way Christ and the church are one. So again I say, each man must love his wife as he loves himself, and the wife must respect her husband. (Ephesians 5:31-33 - NLT).

True intimacy requires you to give of yourself unmasked, uncovered, and unlimited. Each must share certain knowledge that you belong to each other. True intimacy cannot be forced out, driven out, or demanded. It requires freedom of expression and an innate desire to please each other. It is in the nurture of loving relationships that it is actually drawn out.

Though good advice lies deep within the heart, a person with understanding will draw it out. (Proverbs 20:5 - NLT).

Conclusion (Into – Me – See)

"Into-me-see" is a phrase often used in the context of intimacy and relationships that refers to the act of being seen and understood deeply by another person, allowing them to truly know you. It speaks to the need to be seen for who we are, including our vulnerabilities and imperfections, and to be accepted for who we are.

This book is about a journey towards true intimacy with God. We are convinced that this is the level of communion that He desires from those who choose to be committed to Him. Intentionality is crucial for the development of this spiritual bonding and cannot be overemphasised.

It is my expectation and hope that those who desire more from God shall find the pages of this book to be both enlightening and encouraging. The emphasis here is that spiritual intimacy is life-transforming and provides for us a deeper understanding of God and self.

This love relationship that stirs up intimacy grants stability and security, especially in challenging times. The real key to true fulfilment in life is wired to our intimacy with God.

I fully recognise that this volume is by no means exhaustive but that it will primarily serve to either initiate for some and continue for others the conversation concerning intimacy with God as a vital aspect of our prayer life and overall Christian experience.

This book is not just for "professional intercessors" and ministers but rather for the entire Christian community to whom the call to spiritual intimacy beckons. There is no substitute or supplement for knowing God personally. All indeed are welcome to this deeper life experience.

Those with an intimate relationship will easily demonstrate and live a Spirit-filled life that is characterised by the fruit of the Spirit.

Oh, that entire community of believers would press in and grasp this most unique of all Christian experiences. Intimacy with God will indeed break the drought and bring true refreshing to the body of Jesus Christ.

Personal intimacy with God cannot be delegated to another nor should it be relegated to a chore-like activity. The universal call has gone out, and the respondents must heed the call to come. This is not a call for judgment but one for a deeper relationship.

May this work be a guide and a source of inspiration to all those that the Lord has called to Himself.

Other Books by the Author

THE POWER OF THE SECRET PLACE
"The Place of Relationship, Resolution & Revelation."
Valentine A Rodney

LA PERSISTENCIA Desvergonzada
"La audacia de la oración con propósito"
VALENTINE A. RODNEY

SHAMELESS Persistence
"The Audacity of Purposeful Praying"
VALENTINE A. RODNEY

A WAY OF ESCAPE
HOW TO HANDLE THE TESTS AND TEMPTATIONS OF LIFE
Valentine A. Rodney

RECETA PARA RELACIONES SANAS
Guía Práctica Para Superar Las Ofensas

PRESCRIPTION FOR HEALTHY RELATIONSHIPS
A Practical Guide to Overcoming Offences

VALENTINE A. RODNEY
GIVING UP IS NOT AN OPTION
"Persevering Despite Life's Challenges"

SHOW ME THE EVIDENCE
VALENTINE A. RODNEY